Popcorn, Potatoes & Pomegranates

A Grief Encounter

Wes M. Bynum

FLUENCY

TELLING STORIES THAT MATTER

Produced with the assistance of Fluency Organization, Inc.

Design by Inkwell Creative

To Bee

You will always and forever be my best friend,
my wonderful wife,
my stability in ministry, and the love of my life.

I miss you every day.

Love,
Wes

Table of Contents

ACKNOWLEDGEMENTS

I am truly grateful for all the people who encouraged me to write this book. I am thankful for coworkers who showed excitement when I mentioned the possibility of tackling the project. My secretary Courtney for her friendship, faithful support, and extraordinary talent for keeping the office running smoothly even when everything seemed to be "out-of-whack." Also, a special word of gratitude to Lisa LaFrance, RN, who, with a grin on her face and a sparkle in her eye, was constantly asking me, "How's the book coming along?"

My family has been a wonderful source of support. My wife, Betty, has been gracious and understanding throughout the entire process. She unselfishly allowed me to spend a great deal of time and a great number of days alone in my office pounding out words on the computer.

My good friend, Rev. Stacy Sanders, was kind enough to read the chapters as they were written, and he has given me tremendously important feedback along the way. Also, special thanks to Wendy Frizzell, who was willing to proof the text and help me place commas appropriately. I could not have done it without her.

Finally, I give thanks to my wonderful Lord, who has blessed me in so many wonderful ways and for the gentle guidance of the Holy Spirit, who has enabled me to share my story with you, the reader.

FOREWORD

Wes Bynum has brought all of himself to this lovely book: his heart and mind, his intellect and faith, his training as a chaplain and a minister.

In these pages, as Wes shares the very personal story of his own journey through illness, death, and grief, he layers it with words of wisdom from his career, words of comfort from his calling as a man of faith, and very practical advice for those on the same journey.

In bringing all of himself to this heartwarming text, Wes tells a story that is both personal and universal, a wonderful offering from a husband, a minister, and a grief professional.

Nancy Lamar
Vice President of Community Development
The Hospice of East Texas
Tyler, Texas

FROM THE AUTHOR

"The Lord is my shepherd; I shall not want. He maketh me to lie down in green pastures: he leadeth me beside the still waters. He restoreth my soul: he leadeth me in the paths of righteousness for his name's sake. Yea, though I walk through the valley of the shadow of death, I will fear no evil: for thou art with me; thy rod and thy staff they comfort me."
(Psalm 23:1-4)

Grief is a multifaceted response/reaction to loss. When you lose something or someone that you love... you grieve; you respond, you react. Grief is a time of readjustment and redefinition. People grieve the loss of a variety of things: Relationships, Health, Jobs, Financial stability, Independence, Control, Pets, etc. Perhaps the most recognizable grief is that associated with the loss of friends and family, whether it be the result of relocation, separation, divorce, or death. Although the principles of grief can be applied to a variety of life events, in this book my main focus will be on grief as it relates to death. The loss of someone who has been, and will continue to be, a special part of who you are.

Death is a powerful, cold, hard, mysterious word that brings all sorts of images to mind, and yet death is a universal, unique, and natural part of living. No two people die exactly the same, and no two people respond to death (*grieve*) exactly the same. Grief encounters are both individually different and vaguely similar. When grieving the loss of someone special, many people are driven by an innate desire for solace and an assurance that their feelings, emotions, thoughts, and behaviors are "normal." Scholarly facts and academic information about death, dying, and the "process" of grief can be helpful in understanding what they're experiencing, but that is only one side of the coin; *the head side*. On the other side, *the heart side*, people need time to heal and a tender, supportive atmosphere to heal in.

In this book I have done my best to share, not only my own very personal encounter with death and the resulting grief, but to share my heart especially with those of you whose story has not been written the way you had planned. To the brave men and women who have faced disease with strong faith and dogged determination, but without achieving better health or longer life. To let you know that you are not flawed because your prayers were not answered the way you or those around you envisioned. To remind you that walking through the *Valley of the Shadow of Death* is a normal part of living this life.

You are not alone as you walk along the narrow and shadowy trail called *grief.* Rest assured; you are walking on a well-worn path. Others including myself have taken a similar journey. I do not know exactly how you feel, but I know how I felt. I do not know what you are thinking, but I know what I thought. I do not know what battles you are fighting, but I know the ones I fought. And I do not know what lessons you are learning along the way, but I know which ones I learned, and I want to share some of them with you. I want to share the story of my grief encounter with you. It is my desire that in the end you feel ***validated, educated, and inspired to continue living each day with heaven-given Hope!***

Wes M. Bynum

INTRODUCTION

It was Tuesday, September 6, 2011, when it happened. I woke up very early that morning after wrestling with sleep the night before, and the first words to enter my misty mind were: *Popcorn... Potatoes... and Pomegranates.* Lying on my back, I looked up at the ceiling and turned the words over in my brain. Instinctively I knew they were connected to my wife. It had only been two days since she had completed a hard-fought, faith-filled battle with cancer.

Popcorn... Potatoes... Pomegranates, three words that seemed to be random and disconnected... at first, but then they began to speak to me clearly about life and death, loss, and grief. Groggily I got up, walked out of my bedroom, through the kitchen, past the living room, and shuffled into my office. Looking out the window, I could see that the dark black of night was turning into the dull gray of dawn; a signal that the sun would soon shine. I sat down at my desk, picked up a pen, and wrote down the following thoughts.

THOUGHTS:

The process of grief is like living the life of a bag of microwave popcorn

Life before the *"Situation."* You're in the box as usual. You're sitting on a shelf in the pantry minding your own business surrounded by a wide variety of other boxes, bags, bottles, and jars. Each one a different size and shape. Each one unique both outside and inside. You are familiar with the world around you. This is normal "shelf-life" as you know it. But then…

One day you are given an unexpected diagnosis by a doctor, and you discover that you now have a *"Situation"* to deal with. You are yanked from the shelf by a force beyond your control. The box that has defined you is abruptly opened. The clear bag that seals and protects you from exposure is ripped apart, pulled off, and thrown away. And then…

The *"Situation"* becomes a loss. You are tossed into a microwave oven, and you feel all alone. The door is shut. An unfamiliar darkness surrounds you. The silence is deafening. Before you have time to think or adjust to this new place, a blinding light appears. You feel yourself going around, and around, and around again. An obnoxious, unsettling, unrelenting noise begins to ring in your head. Unseen waves of emotional intensity reverberate deep in your heart and mind, causing you to feel like you have never felt before. Things are changing in you and around you. Just when you think that you have found a way to deal with it... things change again. The popping begins. One kernel at a time. One moment, one day, one event, one feeling at a time- pop, pop, pop! You have a vague, instinctive idea that you are going through a process that will leave you forever different. Eventually, the popping begins to slow down. The spinning stops, the light dims, a "ding" is heard, the door to the microwave is opened, and the atmosphere on the outside begins to mix with the atmosphere on the inside. However, the process isn't over because then...

After the *"Situation,"* after the loss, you realize that the door is open, and out of the microwave you go. Freedom! Deliverance! Relief at last! But understand, there is still some heat to deal with. You must be handled with respect because of where you have been and what you have been through. Some settling needs to happen on the inside of the bag. There are still some things that are as they were, but for the most part, everything else in the bag is different. You are different. Are you better? Possibly, but here's a question: Are you going to keep the bag closed and leave your story untold, or will you open up and share with others your very own, very personal, very special *Grief Encounter?*

Remember:

Every grief encounter is different. It begins at

different times for different reasons, it lasts for different lengths of time, and the experiences throughout are unique to the individual. No two "bags" are the same.

The length of the grief encounter is determined by a variety of factors: The power setting (energy level) of the "microwave"; the age of the "microwave"; how many times the "microwave" has been used for this purpose, and what kind of maintenance it has undergone. Also, how often has the door been opened during the process, and how many buttons have been pushed along the way.

And, just be aware that it is not unusual to keep "popping" for a while even though the encounter seems to be over. When you feel that you're "doing good" one day and you're surprised by an unexpected "pop" the next, you're not going crazy and there is nothing wrong with you; it's all a part of the process.

The process of grief is like boiling potatoes.

Have you ever boiled a pot of potatoes? You (normally) pick the pot you want, peel however many potatoes you want, cover them with water, and then set them on the stove to heat. However, it seems that no matter what size of pan or pot you pick, if you're not careful and watchful, you run the risk of "boil-over." A boil-over is a messy thing, and this messy thing is almost a sure thing if you simply put a lid on the potatoes and ignore what's happening on the inside of the pot as the temperature rises.

Often times people try to deal with their grief in much the same manner. They try to put a "lid" on their feelings and emotions. They try not to cry. They work hard to stay busy. They look for ways to avoid the void. They reason with themselves that if they ignore the unpleasantness of grief long enough, it will one day disappear. The truth is grief will always find expression. Sooner or later, in one way or another, and "usually" when you least expect it (or want it), reaction to the loss will manifest itself.

Rather than expending all your energy in trying to resist the natural response to loss, look for positive ways to work with/through it. Lift the lid, stir the pot, and adjust the temperature of the burner if needed. With a little care and a little attention, a messy boil-over may be avoided.

Understand, it's okay to boil potatoes. Just remember when you do, it requires a certain amount of effort. And, if you happen to experience a messy boil-over during the process, wait for the stove to cool down before you start the cleanup; that way there is less risk of burns and scars moving forward.

The process of grief is like eating a pomegranate.

Pomegranates are a wonderful fruit, but you have to be very specific in the way you go about eating one. You can't really just pick it up, rub it on your shirt sleeve, bite a big "hunk" out of it, and expect to enjoy the result. The pomegranate should be properly peeled open and then eaten one or two seeds at a time.

Grieving the loss of someone you love is similar. It's best done one bite at a time, in manageable measure. There is value in the process. It may take longer than trying to finish it off in one "gulp," but the end result will be much more satisfying.

Since the morning that I first penned these thoughts about grief, I have come to realize that they are simply "*some*" among many others that have been written. There have been countless books written on the subject of death, dying, grief, mourning, coping with sadness and loss, etc. The more material that you read, the more you begin to realize that the information is much the same. The words are phrased differently, and the thoughts are framed differently by each writer, but they are all discussing similar ideas/principles.

Popcorn, Potatoes, and Pomegranates: A Grief Encounter is my take on the subject. As you read, take time to absorb the story, as well as the spiritual lessons, grief thoughts, and reflections sprinkled throughout. Without question this is my story, told in my way, but I hope that as you read through the pages you are able to find a level of definition, validation, and comfort. I hope by the time you lay it down you are able to say, "I am glad I took the time to take a look at this book."

Life

By Wes Bynum

The shadows lengthen. The sun moves slowly, and steadily makes its journey to lands far away. The orange red glow begins to melt into shadows and shades of grey. A soft breeze is blowing and the leaves are dancing to its gentle rhythm.

Life

Somehow, in some way, and without clear definition, the light of day is no longer and the darkness of night is now. Why did it have to come? How did it get here? How long will it last? Does anybody notice? What will happen next? Some questions have logical, scientific, absolute answers. Some questions defy our ability to come to any kind of answer at all.

Life

Darkness prevails. It is a time for contemplation and reflection. Truth is hard to accept at times. At some point, thoughts and experiences become memories. Tomorrow holds new hope. Sleep deeply. Rest peacefully. Dream sweetly…

Life

Now open your eyes! Your heart is beating. A sense of anticipation and excitement is in the air. Light has returned. Darkness has gone. The sun is brilliant. The sky is blue. The sweet fragrance of morning is carried along on the wings of the wind. Soft, happy songs of busy birds gently touch the ear. The human soul rejoices.

Life

CHAPTER 1

A RUSH OF ADRENALINE...
A FLOOD OF FEELINGS

Finding the Lump

My heart began to pound as if a steel-headed hammer was beating against a black iron anvil. My stomach began to tighten, churn, and swirl. My knees went wobbly. I found myself swallowing hard and breathing even harder. Adrenaline was racing through my body, making my mind grow dizzy and fuzzy. Feelings flowed like a raging river. Fear; sadness; anger; anxiety; confusion; desperation; pessimism. Faith; hope; love; excitement; determination; optimism. Nothing made sense to me. It seemed as though every feeling that can be felt by man had invaded my life all at once. I was overwhelmed.

It was a Saturday morning, just a normal Saturday morning. The sun was shining. I had enjoyed a couple of cups of coffee. My wife, Bee, had been drinking her *Diet Coke*. Our two grown kids, Ben and Ruth, were both living outside the "nest," but I'm sure they too were having a normal day. However, in a moment of time, the sunshine began to give way to foreboding clouds and "normal" began to morph into "anything but." Bee had stepped out of the shower, slowly walked into our bedroom, and the look on her face was like nothing I had seen before. Bee was a nurse and a smart one, with years of experience. For twenty-five years she had worked for an OBGYN doctor helping countless other women navigate their way through all sorts of medical storms. Now it was her turn. She had found a lump in her breast and both her intelligence as well as her intuition let her know that this was no ordinary lump. She and I and our family would soon find ourselves leaving the clear blue skies of "normal" daily living and entering into the gray, shadow-filled world of Cancer.

The year was 2009. The month was October. Bee and I had been together for a long time. We had met one Sunday morning at Rose Center Assembly of

God church. She was a young nursing student who had recently moved from the rural farm where she had grown up to Tyler, Texas, a city of about 100,000. She had always wanted to be a nurse and bring healing and comfort to hurting people. I was working for my grandfather at the time, who operated an ol' fashioned hardware/furniture store (Pope & Turner, Inc. in Overton, Texas) which he had started in 1938. I wasn't really sure about what I would do in life, but I was keenly aware of a heavenly call in my heart to be a minister of the gospel. I started college and after a few years of soul searching and academics, I ended up with a degree in Business, History/Sociology, and two separate teaching certifications from the State of Texas.

They say opposites attract. I don't know if that is always true, but it certainly was true for Bee and me. We had been brought up in two very different worlds, and yet we soon became close friends, then best friends, and in time, love became the thread that knit our lives together. We were married on June 6, 1981, and happily began living our lives as husband and wife. In time, Bee became a dedicated, skilled nurse. I became a pastor. We were a team. For 28 years we were inseparable soulmates in ministry. She took care of the physical. My role was to care for the spiritual. God blessed our lives and gave us two wonderful children despite mountains of medical problems that should have prevented us from having any children at all. Life was not always perfect, but it was always good. We did not always know all the answers to the questions that we would face, but learned the value of always trusting in the Lord who does. Little did we know that one day we would walk through a valley that would put everything we had believed and experienced to a heart-wrenching, life-changing test.

Bee and I held each other tightly for a long time, the morning "The Lump" was discovered. We spoke in whispers. We shed red hot tears. We took long deep breaths trying desperately to replace the life-giving air that seemed to have been suddenly sucked from our lungs. Time appeared to both slow down and speed up at the same time. Eventually, I got up and finished dressing for the day, but instead of my normal routine, I went out my back door, serviced my chainsaw, strolled down the hill just beyond my house and began cutting down pine trees. It may sound a little strange now, but at the time, it seemed like a perfectly natural thing to do. I was to discover later that it was indeed a very natural thing to do. It was part of my initial response to the news of loss. I was grieving the loss of a familiar way of living. It was my way of reacting to the change that I instinctively knew was coming. I had no way of knowing how much change there would be, nor could I have imagined how deeply I would be affected. It was not possible for me to fathom how many layers of grief there were, nor how heavy each layer would be. However, I knew in my heart and in my spirit that nothing would ever be the same again, not really.

In the book of Exodus, chapter 13 and 14, we find the account of God's chosen people as they walk out of and away from more than 400 years of Egyptian bondage. Spirits are soaring high with excitement; joy is deeply heartfelt, and a sense of fresh anticipation electrifies the air as the Israelites begin their journey toward a land promised to them by God. It is a land of milk and honey (Mmmm)! Step by step they walk across the desert sand, and with each step the memory of their painful past begins to melt into hope-filled thoughts of future life. These people, this generation of "once-were slaves" probably had little to no knowledge about the well-worn ways to get to Canaan, but they were not worried, for the Lord provided them with a cloud to follow during the day and a fire for the night. The Lord had been leading. The children of the Lord had been following. Pharaoh and his army had been staying out of the picture. All was well… until it wasn't.

The song of the day was, "I Am Bound for the Promised Land." However, that song soon turned into the tune, "Gloom, Despair, and Agony on Me," because Pharaoh began to pursue, and the people of God found themselves trapped in the wilderness. They had come to a sea, and there was not a bridge or boat in sight. As the gravity of the situation began to sink in, the folks began to do what most folks would do; they started to gripe and complain and place blame. You know the story. You know that they fussed at Moses for messing up everything, for leading them into the desert to die. "We told you to just leave us alone," they said, "now look what you've done." Feelings of peace and security were quickly evaporating, and a sense of panic and despair began to spread throughout the camp.

In the middle of this crisis, Moses turned to the Lord for direction and the direction the Lord gave was very clear, "I want my children to go forward." The Lord's desire was not for his people to die in the desert.

He wanted them to live in the land of promise. They were not destined to suffer defeat at the water's edge. God wanted them to experience a new level of joy on the other side of the sea! Yes, there was an enemy coming to drag them back into bondage. Yes, they were facing an "ocean of impossibility." Yes, nothing seemed to make any sense at all, not even God's instruction. However, the Lord knew what no one else knew that day... *What He was just about to do!*

The Lord knew about the dangers and fears that his people were facing that day. He knew the width and the depth of the sea in front of them. He knew the size and resolve of the army behind them. God could have simply transported his children from one shore of the Red Sea to the next. God could have sent the enemy scurrying back to where they had come from. God could have led his people around the problem. He could have done any number of other things. Instead, He chose to dry up the bottom of the sea and lead them along a path only He could have provided. As the people moved forward that day, they were reminded with each step that no matter what, The Lord is Faithful.

The day Bee found "The Lump," it seemed as if our world would come to an end. As it turns out, that day was never meant to be the end. It was a new beginning. We were to discover new depths of God's love and faithfulness that we had not imagined before. We were to experience new levels of comfort and care, as the Holy Spirit used family and friends to minister to us in our time of need. And, we were to discover just how deeply the peace that passes understanding is anchored in Christ Jesus our Lord. He could have removed the problem in an instant; instead He chose to walk with us through it and because He did, we learned the honor of living for the Lord... step by step.

COGITATION:

In order to discover new oceans, we must be willing to lose sight of the shore.

A GRIEF THOUGHT

Grief is an individual's response to loss. It is expressed in a variety of ways depending on a variety of variables. People are unique in most every way, and most will experience grief in their own unique way. It is a time-honored principle... there is no "right" or "wrong" way to grieve; there is your way. It turns out that my three-day expedition into the woods with my chainsaw was one of my very own unique ways to grieve. Grief specialists call it, *"instrumental grieving."*

Allow me to explain. If you were to observe people who are grieving and do so using a very broad lens, you would notice two ends of one spectrum. On one end of the spectrum, you would see those folks who are referred to as *"intuitive"* grievers. These are people who have a natural tendency to react to loss by showing their feelings or emotions. They cry (maybe a lot). They talk about how they feel (maybe a lot). They seem to find comfort in the outward expression of what they are experiencing inwardly. These are those who are easily recognized as people who have suffered loss, because you can see the tears and the tissues.

However, there is another end of

the spectrum. On that end you find the **"instrumental"** grievers. These folks are sometimes harder to spot. This group of grievers may not show any recognizable outward sign that a loss has occurred. Because they may not cry (much), it often becomes a point of concern to those closest to them. "My friend just doesn't appear to be grieving," they say (which is code for, "They are not crying or being emotional"). Instrumental grievers have a propensity to work through their grief by *doing* and/ or *thinking, physical activity,* and *problem solving.*

Truth be told, most of us are a combination of "grief types." Whether you tend to be more *"intuitive"* or *"instrumental,"* the key to working through the grieving process is for you to be true to who you are. One is not better than the other. They are simply different ways to achieve the same goal, i.e., **to adjust to living your life as it is *now*, after the loss, as opposed to the way your life *was* before the loss.**

CHAPTER 2

ON A MOUNTAIN
IN THE FOG

The Diagnosis

A fter Bee discovered the lump in her breast that Saturday morning, the rest of the weekend was a blur. I'm sure that I didn't spend the whole time chopping down the forest behind my house. I'm confident that I finished preparations for church services the next day, although I don't remember the details. I can't recall the songs we sang or the sermons I preached that Sunday morning and night. I'm sure the Lord ministered to the people even though whatever my mouth said, my mind was on my wife and children and myself. It was as if I were in a dream. There was a sense that the previous 24 hours had not been real. It felt like my life had somehow transitioned into some sort of slow motion quasi-out of-body experience mode. I thought, "Surely this can't be really happening to us; surely this is all some sort of temporary test that will be quick and painless, without any actual heartache… Surely…"

The day after that Sunday was Monday (I think). That's what the calendar said; that's what common sense said; and that's what the day after Sunday always was. The problem was on this Monday, those things in my world that I took for granted as being normal and common or that made sense were beginning to seem abnormal, uncommon, and nonsensical. Normally, I would have been taking time to pray, read, and study in my office. Normally, I would have been getting started on ideas for the next church service and thinking of people who would need a visit during the week. Normally, I would have been thinking of ways to minister to someone else. However, on this Monday, I found myself going back down the hill with my chainsaw thinking about which trees to cut down and asking God questions… lots of questions.

Bee set off for work on that Monday. She had patients to attend to, and family members of patients to attend to, and documentation on all her "attending" to attend to. As she focused her attention on caring for others, she was doing her best to set up doctor visits and schedule scans and tests for herself. Like me, Bee was starting to realize that her routine was on the verge of becoming *anything-but routine*. She and I were beginning to look for solid answers to fluid questions. We knew future decisions made along this unwelcomed journey would depend on "The Diagnosis."

After physician consultations, and scans, and a biopsy, Bee and I waited impatiently to get the report. Those days were excruciating. It was like listening to the slow, syncopated drip of a leaky faucet. Feelings of apprehension and fear challenged our faith, as we anticipated the next drop of water. We were on edge. When the news did come and my brain began to process the information that my ears were hearing, I felt my pulse begin to race. The tips of my fingers started to tingle. My stomach started to slowly roll deep within my frame. My knees went weak and my feet felt funny. **Cancer!**

Within 24 hours three different doctors had each confirmed the initial diagnosis, we were dealing with Breast Cancer. The lump that Bee had found was no ordinary lump. It was not an innocent benign cyst but a terrible living mass. The physicians, Bee's friends and colleagues, each spoke to us slowly and deliberately as they told us their assessment of our situation. "The cancer is aggressive," they said. "The tumor is irregular," they said. "This needs to be dealt with right away," they said. Three informed medical opinions, all of them in agreement and none of them what we wanted to hear. But, regardless of what we wanted, Bee and I had decisions to make and time was not on our side.

Our son, Ben, was in Henderson, Texas, working as a band director for the school district. Our daughter was in Waco going to school at Baylor working on her degree in Speech Pathology. Somehow Bee and I found the time and the words to share the diagnosis with them. Our kids are smart, and both understood the gravity of the news. Once they heard the diagnosis, Ben and Ruth set out to traverse emotional minefields all their own. There was no doubt, we would walk together as a family through this valley of cancer. Along the way, our children would prove to be tremendous caregivers and solid support for both mom and dad.

As Bee and I were getting the initial reports on the lump in her breast, it was getting close to the middle of October and my birthday. Plans were in place to spend a few days in the mountains of Arkansas to celebrate. Under the circumstances, we debated whether we should take the trip as planned or cancel our reservations and stay close to home. Finally, we agreed that we should go and try to relax. Instinctively, we knew that there we were facing some rough, choppy water. We figured we could use the time to focus, talk through our options, and prepare for the rapids around the bend. So, we packed our bags, loaded up the car, and set out for a short "vacation."

As we drove along, Bee and I kept our cell phones busy, making calls, receiving calls, sending text messages, and receiving text messages. Family and friends were finding out about what we had found out. People responded to the news with prayers, tears, encouragement, instructions/suggestions, and questions (most we could not answer). It proved to be a long drive! Every now and then there would be a lull in the "cell phone storm," and as the highway slipped beneath us, Bee would slip her hand into mine and give it a gentle squeeze. I would fight back tears, swallow hard, and return the gesture. We both knew what those squeezes meant: "I love you and we will make it through whatever we have to go through... *Together*."

We arrived at our destination late in the afternoon,

Mt. Nebo State Park. Exhausted from the miles traveled and the undercurrent of stress that had been flowing in our hearts and minds, we were eager to ascend the hill before us and find a place to rest.

As we made our way up the mountainside, I noticed that the sun didn't seem to be shining as brightly as it had been earlier. The higher we went, the more obvious it was that we were driving into a fog. When we got to the park headquarters located at the top of the mountain, we realized that a cloud had settled in over the entire mountaintop. The fog was so thick you could barely see your feet at the end of your legs. We asked the park ranger how long the fog was expected to last. "Hard to say," was the reply. "Could be an hour, could be a day or so, you never know for sure."

With those welcoming words, we took possession of our key and slowly made our way through the milky haze to find our assigned accommodations. It took some doing, but we eventually found our spot in the fog, parked the car, and got ourselves moved in. As it turned out, we would spend the next three days alone in that one-room rustic cabin, shrouded in fog, poor-to-none cell phone reception, no television, no internet access, no view out of any window or door, and a brand-new diagnosis of cancer!

Struggling with spotty cell service, Bee did her best to get in touch with doctors' offices and schedule follow-up visits. She had to decide what course of action she was willing to take in her "fight against breast cancer." I was doing my best to help her make those decisions and offer as much emotional/spiritual support as I could. As the hours droned by, feelings of frustration; fear; agitation; confusion; sadness; and helplessness swirled around and through us, as if an uninvited ethereal guest had joined us for vacation. At the same time, Bee and I felt our hearts being woven together more tightly than ever. The love that we had shared for nearly thirty years was deepening and growing stronger with each passing moment. The atmosphere inside that cabin was thick and weighty; tender and soft.

The fog on the outside of the cabin was persistent. You could see the movement of a million drops of water as they rode on the wind, and you could feel the moisture on your face, but there was no lifting up, no letting up, no clearing up. There was just fog. A heavy, thick, atmospheric curtain that kept us from seeing little more than shapes and shadows. We could only imagine how beautiful our surroundings might be if the sun were shining. We could only speculate on how spectacular the view would be if only the fog would go away, leave us alone, and let us see!

For two tedious days, I tried to see more than I could see, but it was no use. I wished that I could make the fog disappear. I wished that the fog wasn't so awfully thick. I wished that I was somewhere other than where I was. I wished I could see something, anything, other than that oppressive gray/white, fuzzy, wet, blur. The fog wouldn't go away no matter how much I wished it would. I was feeling trapped by a force beyond my control and I had to get out. On the morning of the third day, I walked out the door determined to take a hike. Visibility was still extremely limited, but my desire to walk around on the outside of the cabin was greater than my willingness to sit still on the inside.

Near the cabin was a trail that roughly followed the contours of the mountaintop. I stepped out the door, took an intentional look around to orient myself, then carefully set out to find the trail. It wasn't long before I was making my way along a narrow, winding path flanked by native grass, small shrubs, rocks, and trees. The fog was still there, but the forest around me seemed to break it up just enough to offer sporadic spottings of the Nature's wonders. Here and there I would spy a spider web heavy laden with tiny droplets of water, gently swaying, slow dancing with the cool damp breeze. Interlaced with the grass at my feet, I spotted some lovely little purple wildflowers, their delicate blooms seemed to say, "Hi" as I passed by. Rolling rivulets of water could be seen, falling carelessly through semi-hidden cracks and crevices in the hill side, tumbling over rocks and forming shallow pools along the trail. Gradually I began to realize that I was surrounded by small wonders and beautiful things… even though the fog still hung heavily in the air.

That afternoon the cloud began to lift off the mountain! In its place, a brilliant sun showered the summit with warmth and light. Vision was restored! We felt free! Bee and I went outside and soaked in the heretofore hidden beauty of the landscape. At one scenic overlook we stood together and looked for a long while down into a picturesque valley. We could see for miles. It was spectacular. However, the longer I looked at the miles of gorgeous countryside that lay before me, the more my mind began to wander back to the fog. I began to contemplate the sights I had seen that morning. I reflected. As I did, I realized that the sun had been shining the whole time; I had just not seen it the way I wanted to. It dawned on me that if the sun had been shining the way I wanted it to, I would have completely missed the wonder of all that I had seen in the fog. I'm sure that I would have been so focused on how far I could see in the distance; I would have overlooked what was close.

Thoughts about *looking* and *seeing*, *sunshine* and *fog*, stayed with me for the rest of the trip. Bee and I continued to wrestle with "The Diagnosis" and tried to plot a course of action that would take us through the dreaded days ahead. All the while, I felt in my spirit that the Lord was doing His best to tell me something. At the time, I couldn't quite understand what He was saying, but later, it came to me: *the importance of small things. The value of acceptance. The joy of finding beauty along the walkway. The peace that comes from embracing what you have and letting go of what you don't.* I recognized the fact that every day is a gift. Yesterday has become a memory. Tomorrow is still an imagination. *Today is Special!* That's what I learned... On a Mountain; In the Fog.

COGITATION:

The little things in life are the great things in life."

— Alexander MacClaren

A GRIEF THOUGHT

Grief does not always begin with death. Often it begins with diagnosis. When you first begin the grief journey it is not uncommon to feel as if you are living in a strange dream. To feel as though you will wake up and everything will be the way it always was. It is also normal to wrestle with a combination of feelings, emotions, and questions at the same time.

The grief experience is not linear. There are no logical, consecutive stages to go through and then cross off the list. Grieving is usually messy. It's sort of like jumping into a washing machine. You are thrown into the tub, you're cramped by the agitator in the middle, the lid is shut, and you are in the dark. A flood comes pouring over you (feelings, emotions, questions). Without warning, you find yourself being moved by a power beyond your control. Around and around. Up and down. Forward and backward. You surge and spin again and again with only short periods of calm between cycles.

In the end you come out much different than the way you went in. Maybe wet and heavy. Maybe knotted and wrinkled. Maybe dizzy and disoriented. Maybe just ready to "dry out." Whatever your description, eventually you realize that you are spending less time on the *inside* of the washing machine and more time on the *outside*. Feelings and emotions are less intense or limiting. You find yourself adjusting to a new way of living. That's grief.

CHAPTER 3

GOING THROUGH THE MOTIONS. WATCHING FROM THE OUTSIDE.

The Information

After we got home from our "mountaintop" experience, Bee and I began the tedious task of educating ourselves about the disease that was destined to dominate our thoughts. We felt compelled to read and retain as much information about the diagnosis as possible. Every lobby, exam room, and check out area that we went to boasted a wide variety of material. There were breast cancer books, breast cancer pamphlets, and breast cancer brochures galore: lying on tables, sitting in clear plastic holders, stacked in cabinets, and squirreled away in drawers. We collected material whenever we were given the opportunity. Each piece of literature described different forms and phases of the disease, and each was written in such a way as to make things easy for the reader to understand (in theory). Doctors, nurses, case workers, and receptionists gave us well-thought-out notebooks and legal documents outlining policies and procedures and protocols. In addition, Bee and I felt compelled to troll the internet in search of even more information regarding such things as: staging, treatment options, cures, and… mortality rates.

Our appetite for breast cancer information was voracious. We wanted to learn more about any medical term or concept that could possibly apply to our case. We wanted to be educated enough to make informed decisions as we pressed through the process. However, for my part, the more I read and studied about cancer, the more I felt disconnected to everyday life. It was like I was living in a dream world, going through the motions in slow motion. It was as if I was watching myself from outside of myself. All along, there was this faint, hard-to-verbalize feeling that if only I could know and understand… something… I could get control of my life again. Surely, one of us would find some information somewhere that would give us some sense of stability.

During this time of information gathering, a mixed-multitude of people began to come out of the proverbial woodwork to tell me a story about someone that they knew who had the "same thing." I'm sure everyone believed that their story would be informative and inspirational, but it wasn't, not really. I didn't want to hear about what someone else did or didn't do. I didn't have the energy or the patience to listen to other people tell me about other people. I grew tired of well-meaning friends and family telling me what to do, where to go, and how to feel. The truth is, the more stories I heard from others and about others, the more isolated and confused I became. I felt frustrated, agitated, disappointed, and helpless. I started feeling guilty because I was feeling selfish. I didn't want people to tell me about them; I wanted to tell them about me. What Bee and I were facing was not the same as what everyone else had faced. This was our challenge, our test, our journey, and I wanted someone to give me the privilege of ownership. Although I was not able to verbalize it at the time, I needed someone to validate my feelings, emotions, questions, and decisions. In a weird sort of way, it was much more encouraging for me to feel that our situation was special, and not just another *"run-of-the-mill deal."*

For weeks, our days were connected by doctor appointments and consultations. It was as if we had been tossed onto a giant medical conveyer belt. We would get up in the morning, get dressed, and go to an office where we would check in with the receptionist and then… sit. We would sit and wait for our name to be called. Waiting rooms offered a variety of options for one's seating pleasure, but most of those options teetered precariously on the border of comfort and were invariably situated in such a way that you could not avoid looking at the ever-present TV monitor mounted on the wall. It seemed to me that wherever we were or whenever we were there, only two types of TV programs were available; News or Soap Opera. Not that it made too much difference because there was never sound with the picture. Around the waiting room (doesn't matter which one) other patients were sitting as well, along with their caregivers. If they weren't staring up at the on-the-wall TV, their heads would be fixed in the down position fiddling with their phones, or they would be mindlessly thumbing through a crumpled magazine that had been handled by hundreds of others before them.

Bee and I would sit and hold hands and, like

everyone else in the room, we would wait for the moment when *the door* that led to *the back* would open. It was always a highlight when that door would open and a nurse with a piece of paper in her hand would call the name of the next patient. Eventually the name that was called would be "Bee" and we would stand up, and make our way through *the door*. As we walked through *the door* the question was always the same, "How are you today?" In my mind I would usually think, "That's a stupid question, given the fact that my wife has cancer." However, my mouth would usually say, "Okay, how about you?"

Once Bee's name was called, and we made it through *the door*, all kinds of things would take place. There was always a scale to "jump up on" so her weight could be determined and duly recorded. Next, blood pressure would be checked and then temperature taken. Afterwards we were either escorted to another, smaller waiting room, or to an exam room. Once we were firmly in place, we would be given the privilege of sitting and waiting... again. Every now and then there would be paperwork to fill out and/or a questionnaire to answer, but mostly we just sat and waited. In those days, we would spend hours waiting in anticipation of spending a few minutes with the doctor. Always hopeful that the information that we would glean from the experience would be just what we needed to make it through the weeks ahead. Sometimes it was, sometimes it wasn't. The doctors were all wonderful. We were treated with kindness, and spoken to plainly. In fact, doctors and nurses would each try to answer our questions, calm our fears, and give us reason to hope. It was *the process* that was excruciating.

After we had visited with the doctor, Bee and I would look at each other, take a deep breath, and follow the nurse to the check-out desk. There, we would be given instructions regarding some other appointment in the future, and I would pick up one more brochure on breast cancer just in case I had missed some shred of information along the way. Then we would leave, go home, and begin to make plans for when we would do it again. This was our daily routine for the first month or so, until Bee finally had surgery. Little did we know that the routine would continue for the next two years as Bee and I walked through the "valley of cancer."

My quest for information continued. In fact, it became a driving force. I wanted the information to make sense. I wanted to believe that a better understanding of the problem would lead to me to a solution, which would lead me back to living life "as usual." I wanted my life to be what it had been before the cancer. I wanted to do what I had always done. I wanted to feel the way I had always felt. I wanted to be what I had always been. I wanted peace. The problem was I was looking for a peace that was based on information and understanding, instead of relying on the **Peace of God,** which goes beyond both. What I wanted was for all my circumstances to change so that I could *feel* different. I wanted to *feel* confident and carefree. I wanted to *feel* brave and courageous. I did not.

Despite how I felt, God was faithful, loving, and kind. The day came, somewhere in the middle of my frenzied search for information, that He reminded me of the words: ***"Let nothing fill you with worry or care. Instead pray, tell the Lord your concerns and allow him to handle the fear that you feel… as you do; the Peace of God, which goes beyond your ability to understand will keep watch over your heart and mind through Christ Jesus."*** *(Philippians 4:6,7 paraphrased) They* were His words, spoken to directly to me when I needed to hear them the most. (Months later, I would discover a deeper definition of the word *"peace."*)

As I reflected on the scripture, I remembered that the peace that Paul spoke of is a peace that is not dependent on circumstance, situation, or my ability to explain everything. This peace doesn't come from information. This peace comes from God. Faith in God. I was also reminded of Isaiah 55:8 *"My thoughts are not your thoughts, neither are your ways my ways. For as the heavens are higher than the earth, so are my ways higher than your ways and my thoughts than your thoughts."* And too Isaiah 26:3,4 *"Thou (Oh Lord) will keep him in perfect peace, whose mind is stayed on thee: because he trusts in thee. Trust ye in the Lord forever: for in the Lord JEHOVAH is everlasting strength."* It was as if the Lord was saying to me, "It's okay to look for information regarding things you don't know, but as you look, don't forget what you do know."

COGITATION:

At the close of day, shadows lengthen and darkness falls. At times, it may be tempting to run westward and chase after the setting sun. However, it is in facing eastward and plunging into the darkness, that we discover the full light of tomorrow.

A GRIEF THOUGHT

One of the most challenging aspects of the grieving process is adjusting to change. Most people are uncomfortable with change to one degree or another, especially when it occurs without their input or consent. When change comes crashing into our lives because of circumstances beyond our control, it can leave us feeling dizzy, disorganized, disoriented, disbelieving, disturbed, discouraged, dismayed, dismantled, disheveled, and maybe even highly discombobulated. Stability becomes our priority.

Stability comes by choice not chance. You probably didn't choose to lose that special someone in your life. If you're like most people who are grieving, you probably have a hard time knowing when you are going to be flooded with thoughts, emotions, or feelings (let alone some combination of all three). More often than not, they seem to come when you least expect them. You can't always choose when "grief" will hit, but you can choose how to respond when it does.

There is an old question: "How do you eat an elephant"? The answer... one bite at a time. In the world of grief, the best way to make it through is... one choice at a time, one decision at a time. Each day brings new challenges, so find ways to make little choices that will help you overcome the challenge in front of you each day. It may be that you choose to go to the grocery store. It could be that you choose to put on clothes rather than pajamas. Your choice may be to get out of the bed. On the other hand, you may choose to stay in bed and not do anything, to slow down and pamper yourself. Whatever you need to do for you to get through the grief you are facing, **choose to do it!** Give yourself permission to feel what you feel and to respond to how you feel the way you choose to do so. If you don't, then prepare to float through the day carried along on the fickle breezes of feeling and emotions.

When you make a **choice** (and at least make an attempt to do what you've chosen to do), that leads to a sense of control. You made a decision. You did what you decided to do… **Control.** With that sense of control, comes a sense of confidence. That inner voice that says, "What I have done, I can do again" … **Confidence.** Finally, with that confidence comes a sense of stability. That feeling that you get when you are not rocking, rolling, swinging, or swaying… **Stability. (Choice-Control-Confidence-Stability.)**

Every day that you live (even if you're living with grief), you are given the opportunity to make new choices. Your choices will be influenced by both the information that you have, as well as your understanding of that information. Also, your faith will influence the choices you choose to make. Be encouraged to make the effort to make the choices that will help you move in the direction you want to go. Change can be very unsettling and confusing and destabilizing. However, Stability is not out of the question; it just comes by **choice, not chance**.

REFLECTION:

Leap off the Lawn Chair... Fly!

One spring day two birds showed up on my back patio and began making my home their home. I watched for weeks as Mr. and Mrs. Robin built their nest in an old wrought-iron bird cage hanging on a crooked hook just outside my window. It was fascinating to see sticks and straw and grass come together to form a cozy, "twiggy" abode. Eventually, the day came when the construction came to an end. The nest was ready and Mrs. Robin settled in to sit while

Mr. Robin stood guard.

She sat faithfully and with purpose day and night. She sat through days of wind and rain. She sat through calm, peaceful days as well as days filled with flurries of outside activity. She continued to sit, even when the first spring rumblings of the lawn mower whirred and whined, very loud and very close to the nest. I noticed that no matter what the day was like, Mrs. Robin remained loyal to her mission: to bring life into this world.

All of her sitting paid off. One day Mr. and Mrs. Robin were joined by three little Robin kiddos. They were very small and kind of fuzzy and very, very hungry. They had some growing to do and the parents knew it. Thus, began the feeding process. It was constant. Mr. and Mrs. Robin busied themselves searching for food for their little Robin family and delivering their findings to outstretched necks and wide-open mouths. The scene was repeated again and again and again. The little birds began to grow.

Eventually the nest that had been so carefully built by their parents became too small for the three "Robin kids." The baby birds had been changing right before my eyes, and it was almost time for them to leave. The day of their departure was lacking in fanfare or fuss. I simply looked out the window, and they were gone. As I said my goodbyes, I pondered the miracle of life.

The next morning, I woke just before sunrise. After sleepily making a pot of coffee, I slipped outside, located a lawn chair on the back patio, and sat down to drink. As I sipped the hot, rich brown liquid, I noticed something on the lawn chair next to me. In the dim grey of the early morning, I couldn't quite make out what it was, but whatever it was, it was very small and very still.

As the sun continued to wake up the day, the light grew brighter and I realized that it was one of the "Robin kids." He/

she had left the nest the day before, but obviously had not gone too far. There was no sound to be heard, nor any movement to be seen from the fledgling as it sat there facing the nest that had once been its home. The safety and security that the nest had provided the day before was no longer the same. Things had changed indeed.

As I continued to watch the bird on the back of the lawn chair, Mrs. Robin flew down from a nearby tree and perched next to her offspring. I remained very quiet and tried not to move as I watched the familial scene play out only a few feet away. The mother faced her prodigal child and began to hop and chirp on the back of the lawn chair. Next, she fluttered her wings, chirped a little more and flew away. I'm not positive, but I think momma was reminding her little one that things in his life were different now. The nest he was looking at, and wishing to return to, was no longer the place for him to be. It was as if I heard her say, "There's a big world to explore, fresh worms to find, new robins to meet, and new nests to build." In other words, "Little one, you have a life to live beyond this nest!"

I put the coffee cup to my lips; I took another sip, and without warning, the little bird spread its little wings, made a mighty leap into the air, and flew away.

As I reflect on that spring morning scene, I realize: That is life... that is living... that is, how it is after you've left the nest. Even if you could go back and crawl in, you would quickly realize that nothing is the same as before. There are life-changing events that take place in all of our lives that make things different. So, remember, every day is a new day and every sunrise is an invitation to live.

You have a choice to make: remain motionless, staring at where you have been, or take one more look, spread your wings, and **Leap off the lawn chair... FLY!**

CHAPTER 4

FEAR!

The Surgery

Bee and I had spent weeks visiting with doctors, conferring with specialists, and listening to family and friends. We had gathered information and had been given advice. We had prayed and asked the Lord for His wisdom and direction. We did everything that we knew to do. Finally, we made a choice. Bee was going to undergo double mastectomy surgery. It was to be done by one of the most experienced and knowledgeable breast surgeons in the State of Texas, at Baylor Hospital in Dallas. As part of the procedure, a leading cosmetic surgeon was scheduled to join the team and introduce two breast implants into Bee's body.

The day before the surgery, we packed the car, closed the door to our home in the country, and began to make the trip to Dallas. The drive was not too far, only about 80 miles, but it seemed to take us a long, LONG time to get there. As the highway silently slipped beneath the hood of the car, neither Bee nor myself talked much. Bee was in full blown nurse mode, a thousand different clinical scenarios racing through her sharp mind. As usual, I was mentally processing a complex mixture of feelings, emotions, and faith. I was trying to figure out how to be both a supportive pastor and a loving husband to the one person in the world who meant most to me: Bee.

Once we arrived at our destination, we were dutifully checked in and shown to our room. We got unpacked and then tried to settle down and settle in for what the next day would bring. However, the current of events and undertow of emotions was far too strong for either of us to get much rest that evening. Before the sun would have a chance to rise and shine over a new day, the surgery would be underway. The clock was ticking. I was beginning to find out what it's like to look deeply into darkness and be touched by the callused fingers of fear.

As anticipated, early the next morning, gowned "representatives" from the O.R. came to greet us. They checked and double checked who Bee was and what procedure she was expecting to have done that day. After a steady stream of hospital personnel had come through the door, we were visited next by an angel. Our daughter, Ruth, had driven up from Waco that morning. She had made room in her busy class schedule at Baylor University to be with her mom and dad. Tears of joy and gratitude were shared by the three of us. Bee had been worried about the prospect of me sitting alone during the surgery. I had been worried that I might need help hearing, understanding, and remembering what the doctor would say after the surgery. And, I think that Ruth instinctively knew what her mother and father were worried about.

Bee was lying in her bed and was just beginning to relax when two nurses came into the room and announced that it was "time." Monitors that had been keeping track of her pulse rate, blood pressure, oxygen levels, and what not throughout the night were quickly checked and then unplugged. Time had been oozing by at a snail's pace, but now it seemed like the snail had slipped on its sneakers and things were speeding up—*fast*. I could barely get my brain to hold on to what was going on as we walked out the door. Bee, Ruth, and me—the three of us together—were walking quickly and shaking ever-so-slightly, as we drew closer and closer to Pre-Op.

As we moved down the corridor, the atmosphere felt coldly antiseptic, and the feeling was exacerbated by the stark florescent lights that were shining from the ceiling. I walked alongside my wife and held her hand. Ruth followed close behind. One nurse was pulling the bed, another pushing, and as they did, the wheels made a gentle swishing-sticky kind of noise. In addition, I noticed that the well-waxed floors were causing our shoes to make a sort of muffled, squeaking sound. I'm sure it was quite a sight to see; our little swishing-sticky, squeaky parade marching down the hospital hallway. It might have been comical if it hadn't been for the fact of where we were going and why.

Finally, we came to the entrance of a restricted area and the procession paused. I bent down and kissed my wife. A steaming hot lump filled my throat and a rush of blood raced through my veins as I watched her disappear through wide double-doors. There was a sign on each of them that read, "No Admittance" ... "Authorized Personnel Only"! She was beyond my reach. Ruth was with me, but I felt strangely alone. I was afraid. It was not pleasant.

The doctor had informed us that the surgery would take at least 3-4 hours, so Ruth and I decided to go have breakfast at a little pancake place located just across the street from the hospital. It was a busy eatery, filled with a motley assortment of business men and women dressed in freshly pressed suits, deftly juggling cups of coffee and laptop computers. Alongside them, judging from the number of scrubs and name badges that I saw, was an undeniable representation of the medical community. Ruth and I were seated among the "morning meal melee." The food was good, the coffee was hot, and the conversation was focused on Bee. We talked about the cancer. We talked about all the information that had been given. We talked about the surgery. We talked about possible outcomes. We talked about what life was and how it might be.

After a while we thought it best to get back to the hospital. So, we walked past the cars in the parking lot outside the restaurant, crossed the busy downtown Dallas street, and then walked past the cars outside the hospital. We entered through the front doors of the building and made our way to the small area where we were given permission to wait. And so, we sat there, and paced up and down there, while we waited for the surgeons to do what it is surgeons do.

The longer our vigil went, the more things began to get fuzzy. I tried to read the Gideon Bible that was lying on a table in one corner of the room. I couldn't. I tried to read a magazine that I found in a rack on a wall. I couldn't. I tried to watch the TV mounted on the wall. I couldn't. Time was not standing still (*for time stands still for no man*), but it sure felt like it had slowed down to a snail's pace... again! From time to time I would get up, leave the waiting room, and walk back in the general direction of the two double-doors that had those signs hanging on them. I must have walked for miles that day, but I never made it very far.

As a minister, I had been with countless people on countless occasions like this one. I had been in hospital waiting rooms all across the state of Texas, Louisiana, Arkansas, New Mexico, and Oklahoma. I had been with friends and family and church folk. I had been with people that I had known well and with others that I had barely known at all. I had felt the tension as minutes turned into hours and the question on everyone's mind was, "Will 'they' be okay?" I knew what this experience was like. Except... NO... this was different!

Ruth and I were given regular updates on Bee's

condition by the O.R. staff. With each call there was a temporary sense of relief, and the tension that came from waiting and wondering would ease... a little. However, as the minutes slowly turned into hours, and the hours began to add up to a number higher than anticipated, it was difficult to dismiss feelings of fear and dread.

After about an hour or so of waiting room "drama," I looked up and saw a familiar face coming around the corner. It was my best friend, Rev. Albert Cortez, pastor of Family Life Assembly of God Church in Katy, Texas. He had driven close to 260 miles that day just to offer emotional and spiritual support to me and my family. I had not expected him to come, but it was an absolute blessing that he did.

I had first met Albert while I was pastoring my first church, Rose Center Assembly of God in Tyler. It was a Wednesday evening, and I was preaching. He came in and sat on one of the pews toward the back. He was tall, with black hair and an olive complexion, and was well dressed. Later on, I found out that he was originally from New York City and had been raised by his Puerto Rican mother and grandmother in the Bronx. He had been living in Tyler, working as Crusade Director for an internationally known evangelist and attending one of the largest churches in the city. Not long after that first meeting, Albert told me that he had felt led of the Lord to start attending Rose Center. (I had heard this kind of spiritual talk before from other people and took his words with a grain of salt.) As it turned out, he was right, and soon he became a tremendous asset to the church and wonderful friend to me.

When Albert first rounded the corner, I was surprised to see him. After exchanging the usual greetings, we sat down and continued to wait for news about Bee. It wasn't long before I began to grow vaguely aware of a strange feeling beginning to creep over me. I had spent most of my life caring for other people and supporting other people. It was odd and awkward for me to be on the receiving end of that same kind of care. I didn't know exactly how to react or accept what was being offered to me, but somehow, I knew that it would be important for me to figure it out. I needed to learn how *to give myself permission to receive* from others.

Albert's arrival at the hospital and the time he took to minister to Ruth and me was a heartfelt reminder of the value of friendship and the power of presence. As a friend, he was there to listen. He let me talk when I needed to talk and to say what I needed to say. And, perhaps even more important, he let me be quiet when I needed to be quiet. He was there. He was present. He was with me where I was. I fought fear all day, but I did not fight alone. My friend showed up to support me; in doing so, it made me realize just how timely and personal God is. His presence was warming, consoling, reassuring, and comforting. He had not come with a busy agenda; he had come with an open heart.

By the end of the day and after more than six hours of surgery, Bee was wheeled into the recovery unit. We continued to wait for another hour or two. Late in the evening, she was brought back to the same room she had left that morning. We met her there. She was in tremendous pain. She was terribly sick. She was in for a rough night. There had been complications. Things unforeseen and out of the ordinary had occurred throughout the day. The cancer that had invaded Bee's body had done so with unusual ferocity. This cancer did not follow "normal" protocol. This cancer did not "color within the lines." Bee's story would not be told with a happy smile holding pink balloons. It would be told with faith and determination, holding on to God's unchanging hand.

We worked for a long time, trying to get Bee comfortable. As we did, I was reminded of the fact that things don't always go "right" for everybody. Life doesn't always turn out the way you **wish, will, or want it to**… even for the child of God. There may be times when you find yourself dealing with "stuff" that you don't want to deal with. There may be a day when you wake up and realize that you're stuck on the muddy bottom of some deep, dark pit. To make things worse, you know that you don't deserve to be there (Jeremiah 38)! The good news is no matter where you are, or what you're facing, *the Lord knows* where you are and what you're facing! He can get you out of whatever mess you may be in, *or*, He can simply send you comfort and encouragement in the middle of your mess. Either way, the Lord has a way of touching your life in such a way as to change your life forever.

The entire time Bee and I were at that hospital, the Lord was touching my life in a life-changing way. The hour grew late, and Ruth had to drive back to Baylor. Albert had to head back to Houston. Bee and I were left alone. The night wore on, and I grew very weary. Worry kept me awake. Fear had not left. Questions about the future flooded my mind. I held tightly to every biblical promise I could think of. In the middle of all this, the Lord was trying to teach me a valuable lesson: **Faith is not the absence of fear; it is an absolute trust in God.** This lesson would become a solid truth that would provide me firm footing for the slippery slopes ahead.

COGITATION:

"Many are the afflictions of the righteous: but the Lord delivers them out of them all" (Psalm 34:19).

Before you can be brought out of something, you must first be in something. There's no promise that keeps us from getting into a predicament. However, we do have a promise that keeps us from having to stay in it.

A GRIEF THOUGHT

Grieving times are often lonely times. Lonely times are often associated with feelings of isolation. Isolation conjures up thoughts of punishment, confinement, imprisonment, limited contact, and limited communication. Feelings of fear, anxiety, confusion, frustration, anger, guilt, heartache, helplessness, and hopelessness. These feelings can be very much a normal part of your "grief world."

Think about this when you think about how you feel: Feelings **describe** us, they do not **define** us. Feelings provide us with a general **description** of our emotional condition at any given moment on any given day. They do not provide a **definition** of our character. If you live, you feel. It's okay to feel what you feel.

If you are feeling lonely after a loss, and you're looking for ways to lessen that feeling, *give yourself permission to be with other people.* Also, *give other people permission to be with you.* On the other hand, if you want to be alone for a time to collect your thoughts and regain your energy without feeling that you have to "entertain" someone, *give yourself permission* to do that. Everyone views this subject differently. Think about what "fills" you, as opposed to what "drains" you. Remember, there is a difference in feeling lonely and being alone.

Whether you are by yourself or with other people, when you are grieving you are liable to be reminded of who is not with you. (When you go to a restaurant you have to admit that you're a party of one. Or, you are the third, fifth, … seventh wheel; you're the odd man/woman out.) That is awkward. That is normal. That is to be expected. Rather than trying to "not think" about the one who is not with you, embrace those thoughts, hold them close to your heart, and cherish them as you live your way through each day.

The reality of Bee's surgery and the complications that followed brought me face-to-face with a feeling of fear that was unlike anything I had ever experienced. It was both numbing and spine-tingling at the same time. My initial response was to turn inward and politely refuse most help offered from the "outside." However, the intensity of my emotions was exacerbated by my "self-isolation." Later in the journey, I began to discover the importance of allowing myself the privilege of receiving support from friends and family. The more I let other people in to my world of grief, the less I felt alone and afraid.

CHAPTER 5

OH, TO NAIL JELL-O TO A WALL... ANY WALL

The Treatment

The following day we were told by the lead surgeon that, even though the procedure had taken more time than expected, a long hospitalization would not be necessary, and so we prepared to go home. Various members of the "medical community" came to our room to have us sign forms and to give us instructions regarding such things as: wound care, pain management/medication, normal recovery expectations, and standard follow up protocol. By the time the afternoon had arrived, Bee and I found ourselves on the Interstate heading for home!

The farther I drove, the more anxious and uneasy I began to feel. "Things" seemed disjointed, disconnected, and out of place. I kept trying to convince myself that it was normal for me to feel this way, but self-arguments were falling short. My thoughts kept going back over the chain of events that had so quickly redirected our lives. Cancer had not conquered, but it had certainly invaded, and now, battle lines were being drawn. It was intimidating to think that the "Fight" against this dreaded disease was in many ways just beginning, and the stakes were as high as they could get... Life or Death. Every so often, I would glance to my right and see Bee trying to make the best of the long, bumpy ride home. The doctor had given Bee something for pain before the trip, but I could tell by the furrow on her forehead that she was drawing from her deep well of willpower to remain upright as she rode along.

By the time we pulled into our driveway it was obvious that Bee was in misery. I helped her from the car, walked with her into the house, and got her settled in the bed. A big, hopeful part of me wanted to believe that by coming home and by surrounding ourselves with familiar sights, sounds, and smells, everything would be okay. However, it wasn't long before Bee called me to the bedside and asked for her thermometer. I went to where she kept her "nurse stuff," rummaged around a bit, and found the instrument she had requested. She took her own temp and found an elevated fever. She also began noticing that the skin around her incisions was beginning to show the red, tell-tale signs of inflammation/infection. A number of very uncomfortable hours crept by as we tried to bring her body back into balance, but in the end, it was decided that a trip to the local ER was in order. As it turns out, this trip to the hospital would only be one among many that we would make over the coming months.

We spent the next week or more in the hospital receiving I.V. antibiotics to help quell infection. Finally, the day came that the doctors felt confident enough about Bee's bloodwork that we were allowed to go home, but instead of coming to an end, our clinical roller-coaster ride was just getting started. It was mid-November 2009, and Thanksgiving was quickly approaching. However, my attention was not on "turkey and dressing"; it was on Bee's health. It was time to contact the local oncologist, schedule an appointment, and begin discussing follow-up options for treating the cancer. It was time to meet with the local cosmetic surgeon who would monitor the progress of

Bee's recovery and make the necessary adjustments to the breast implants. In addition, because of her "run-in" with infection, now there was an infectious disease specialist to visit on a regular basis.

We muddled our way through the holiday season, and Bee continued to have problems recuperating. Her immune system had been compromised by the infection and her strength was low. However, both of us were determined to press forward, and by January 2010, we had a treatment plan in place. For the next 12 months we would wage war against an elusive, frustrating, and deadly enemy.

Every day provided a new challenge. It seemed like we were constantly being given hard-to-comprehend information, hard-to-embrace options, and then asked to make complex, weighty decisions. It was as if we had fallen into a well-camouflaged pit of "medical quicksand," and we were trying desperately to keep from being sucked into suffocating oblivion. Every step we took felt awkward and unbalanced, hesitant, and uncertain. With each new sunrise, there was a deep desire to hear words of encouragement and hope. Too often, each new sunset left us with only vague ideas and unanswered questions.

Together, for the majority of 2010, we faced raging

fevers, dealt with deadly infections, and processed news of "lymph-node involvement." We experienced multiple rounds of intense chemo-therapy, and survived low white blood cell levels again and again. We endured multiple hospitalizations, multiple surgeries, miles of tubing, endless drains, constant wound care, and untold numbers of needles along the way. The treatment was anything but smooth, and we were looking forward to the day when life would make sense again. However, at this point, no matter what we did, where we went, who we spoke to, or how hard we tried, nothing appeared clear. Nothing seemed solid. Our lives were consumed by shifting shadows and unfiltered frustration. For me, it was like trying to "nail Jell-O to a wall" … regardless of how hard you concentrate or hit the nail, the Jell-O refused to stay stuck!

Despite the challenges we faced that year, there were some heartwarming lessons that we learned along the way. Perhaps the greatest, most endearing lesson involved the people that joined us along the journey. Medication was helpful, information was valuable, but it was the people who made the process bearable. Our family and friends brought us food and took turns staying with Bee as I continued to pastor the flock I had been called to shepherd. People from our church, as well as people from other churches around the state, called to pray for us or sent cards to encourage us along the way. Unforgettable were the primary care doctors, oncologists, infectious disease specialists, general surgeons, and plastic surgeons, each of whom left a lasting impression on our lives. Physician assistants, RNs, LVNs, phlebotomists, pulmonologists, social workers, case workers, and aids; they all touched us deeply, in special ways. Mitch, Dale, Svetislava, Laura, Thomas, Steven, Donna, Brandi, Heidi, Lisa, and Dawn... some of the names, of some of the **people who helped make the treatment process bearable.**

COGITATION:

Faith is not found in comfortable surroundings or acquired according to plan. Faith is forged in fires unforeseen and shaped on anvils unexpected.

Jesus said, "Peace I leave with you, my peace I give unto you... let not your heart be troubled, neither let it be afraid." (John 14:27)

Treatment days were trying days. Hours spent in a sterile room, surrounded by other cancer patients, each one "hooked up" to an I.V., waiting for his or her personal chemo concoction to slowly flow down the tube and into their veins. The patients sat in recliners designed especially for the task at hand and were made as comfortable as possible, given the circumstances that brought them there. Next to the recliner, a small chair or stool was provided for family members or friends to sit on while the treatment was being administered. Nurses stayed busy buzzing about, checking monitors, and would occasionally pause to hover over a patient who showed unusual signs of fatigue or nausea. The ever-present TV was available to watch as the hours dripped by.

My life was changed forever on one of Bee's treatment days.

The day started out as any other day. As she got herself ready to make the trip into town, Bee felt weak and slightly nauseated. Both the sickness *and* the treatment for the sickness had taken a toll on her health, but my wife was determined to get beyond the disease that was draining life from her body. I drove to the front entrance of the oncology clinic, helped Bee out of the car, helped her into a wheelchair, and rolled her into the building where she would be warm as she waited for the chemo to begin. There was a cold, harsh wind blowing, and Bee was frail.

Getting back into the car, I shifted from "park" into "drive" and headed for the crowded parking lot. I drove slowly, looping my way through the lot looking for a parking space. As I searched for a spot, I remember thinking to the Lord: "How do I pray for my wife? What should I say when I pray? What is the right combination of words? What order do I put them in? What phrase is the phrase that will guarantee my prayers will be heard? What formula do I use? What recipe do I use? What ingredients are the right ingredients? How can I work up my faith to the level needed for a miracle to take place?"

As the questions filled my mind, my heart became heavy and an overwhelming, all-consuming burden engulfed me. I thought, "It's my responsibility to believe and pray 'the right way' so that Bee will be healed. It's my responsibility to make sure there will be a positive and powerful testimony to share with others after all is said and done. Countless people, from all over the world, are praying for my wife, and I must make sure that I do everything 'right' so that their prayers will be answered."

The more I thought about it, the more I could feel an emotional pressure mounting inside me. Spiritual anxiety was growing. I began to feel smothered by uncertainty. I felt threatened by forces beyond my control. I felt like I had come to an end. Looking ahead, I could only see long, dark shadows of disappointment and an endless ocean of unanswered questions.

My mind continued to swish and swirl, and then… I broke, and I began to weep. Gripping the steering wheel like a vice, I cried out, *"Lord, I don't know! I don't know what is right! I don't know what to do. I don't know what to pray. And, I don't know what you are going to do. I don't know if you are going to heal Bee or not. But what I do know is:* ***I… LOVE… YOU… and, I TRUST YOU!"***

Those words came gushing out of my mouth like water from a fire hydrant, and as soon as I said them, I was completely consumed with **Peace!** The **Peace** the Lord spoke of in John 14. It was more than a feeling. It was something beyond my ability to analyze or explain. It went deeper than all the sermons that I had preached or songs that I had sung over the years. The **Peace** that filled my life that day was saturating, strengthening, solidifying, powerful, and foundational. Calm settled into my heart, forcing fear to vanish in an instant, and faith to rise.

With one heartbeat, my love *for* Him and my trust *in* Him were welded together. From that moment on, I realized that He was in absolute, complete, and comprehensive control of my life. I knew that whatever happened to Bee, God would never be anything less than what he had always been... *all-powerful, all-knowing, always present and always loving. I was free!* Free to keep my faith in God and free to focus on Bee. The future did not depend on my strength, wisdom, or ability. All I had to do was love the Lord and trust Him to do what needed to be done.

Warm tears were still washing my eyes when I finally found a parking space. After I parked the car, I made my way into the clinic where I found Bee still sitting in the wheelchair. She was waiting for her name to be called and the next round of chemo to begin. Eventually, another treatment got underway. The I.V. was started, the drug began to drip, and we waited to see what the effect would be this time. Things around me seemed the same. Things within me were forever different.

My life was changed forever on one of Bee's treatment days, because on that day I made sure God had all my Love, and in return, God made sure I had all His Peace!

A GRIEF THOUGHT:

Death and/or loss affects people in a variety of ways, on multiple levels at the same time. Emotions are probably the most readily recognizable reaction to loss. However, emotions (or lack thereof) are only part of the multifaceted ways people experience grief. Grief can also very naturally influence us physically, cognitively, socially, and philosophically/theologically.

Physical responses to grief may include, but are not limited to, such things as: restlessness, disrupted sleep patterns, altered eating habits, feeling shaky, increased heart rate, tightness in the chest or throat, loss of energy, and gastrointestinal disturbances (I call it... *"Gastro-Interruptus"*...). Because many of these physical responses to loss are so similar to actual medical conditions, it is highly recommended that you consult with a physician and communicate with them openly.

When dealing with loss, some people

have problems with concentration. They find it difficult focusing on or finishing a task that "normally" would be routine. Reading becomes a chore. Making decisions, even simple ones, causes major anxiety and stress. Some people catch themselves thinking constantly about their loved one and/or the events associated with the loss (referred to as, "loss centered thinking," which is not unusual). Feeling as if they are losing their grip on reality or are going "crazy"; wandering aimlessly around the house. Seeking to place blame for the loss. These are often common elements of a cognitive response to grief.

Sometimes social patterns change. There may be those who lose interest in social activity for a time. Others may find themselves constantly on the lookout for interaction with other people. Feeling as though they will be a burden or a "drag," some may alter their behavior and isolate themselves from friends and family.

Grief can, and often does, affect us on a philosophical or theological level as well. Major illness, disease, the process of dying and death, these life experiences have a way of making us think about things we are not used to thinking about and asking questions that we may not be comfortable asking. For instance, in grief, it is very common to ask the question "Why?" To mull over a variety of scenarios like: "What if…" or "Maybe I should have…" or "If only this had happened…" This train of thought can be very awkward and unsettling for someone who has been taught all their life that they should never question. Some may find themselves questioning long held spiritual beliefs or struggling with the idea of blaming God for an outcome. This is not usual, but it can lead to deep feelings of anxiety, guilt, fear, or anger.

Remember, there is no one thing or combination of things that you must do or experience in order to grieve appropriately.

And too, remember, the influence grief has on an individual goes beyond feelings and emotions. It has the potential of naturally affecting us: physically, cognitively, socially, and philosophically/theologically.

REFLECTION:

A Moment (Well) Taken

It was the holiday season and, as usual, I was on my way to make my way through another busy day at work. The traffic was normal. The pressure I felt as I mentally ran down the list of my "to do's" for the day was normal. In fact, everything appeared to be fairly normal... until I happened to glance down and noticed the time. As the numbers registered on my brain, I realized that I was just a little early for a meeting. And then it happened, for some inexplicable reason I pressed the brake pedal, turned on my turn signal, and pulled into a parking lot. I had passed by this parking lot every day and hardly given it a second thought. On this day, however, I found myself in it. I came to a stop; I put the car in park; I turned off the radio; I turned off the engine, and I took a deep breath.

Slowly, I lifted my eyes to look past the dashboard and there it was, right in front of me... a beautiful morning sunrise. The sky was spectacular! Above the cars and trucks and SUVs and trailers and headlights and taillights... above the buildings and the billboards, the sun was rising in the east and grey clouds were floating by, changing shapes at the whim of the cool winter breeze that blew. As they moved ever-so-slowly, the sun beyond seemed to squeeze its golden rays through the shadows. The sun with all of its brightness and brilliance seemed a warm and welcomed friend, but the clouds added something special to the canvas as well. They added shape, shadow, depth, and perspective. The grey clouds of the morning, gently rolling past the rising sun, reminded me of the mystery of life, the privilege of hope, and the power of peace.

Oh... to pull over from time to time (especially during the busy holiday season) and shift into park, turn everything off just for a moment. Then to lift up our eyes and see the wonder of what is, more often than not, right in front of us. There are thoughts to think, mysteries to contemplate, and there is hope to embrace... just beyond the dashboard and above the buildings and the billboards.

If you will take the time to pull over every now and then, you too may just find that it is... A Moment (Well) Taken.

CHAPTER 6

A BIT OF AN AFTERTASTE

The Recovery

The *Random House College Dictionary* that has been a part of my library since high school defines the word "**aftertaste**" as: "*the remaining sensation following an unpleasant experience...*"

Bee was scheduled to receive her last chemo treatment in the late summer/early fall of 2010. We had been traveling along the cancer trail for a year, and the path had been filled with a plethora of unexpected twists, turns, and detours. We had slogged our way through swamps filled with pain and nausea. We had picked our way along steep cliffs of frustration and fear. We had breasted our way through thick, tangled jungles of confusion and disappointment. We had also discovered scenic overlooks along the way that provided us opportunity to pause and reflect on the fragile beauty of life. On this "last chemo" day, we saw *the trail of treatment* come to an end, and we began to walk in a different direction… *the road to recovery.*

The staff at the cancer center were eager and excited to see us when we arrived for Bee's last appointment. Everyone had been super supportive through some very difficult days, and they understood that this day was special. As Bee was being "hooked" up to her last I.V. and the last round of chemo began to spread through her veins, she closed her eyes to rest. I watched her for a while; the lady I loved, the incredible woman who had fought fear faithfully, battled pain bravely and stared down death defiantly. I began to think about how different life had become since the day "*the lump*" was first found, and I wondered how different life would be in the days ahead.

Finally, the last drop of *chemo cocktail* made its way down the long plastic tube that led to Bee's body, and it was time to get "unhooked." It didn't take long. I gently helped Bee to her feet, and we slowly walked toward the exit for the last time. As we moved closer to the door, we gave heartfelt hugs and said our goodbyes to nurses and other clinic staff who had become our friends. One of the nurses asked Bee if she wanted to "ring the bell." This was in reference to a large brass bell mounted near the entrance of the treatment room. Patients who successfully completed their chemo treatments were given the opportunity to make the bell ring in recognition of their triumph. Bee declined. It wasn't because she felt defeated or depressed, but simply because she knew that there was still work to be done. A battle had been fought. The war continued. Because of the course the cancer had already taken, and the complications encountered along the way, chest radiation would not be a future option. So, instead of thinking about what could happen, or what might take place at some point, Bee and I simply began to focus on living one day at a time.

As is common in life, some days were "good," some days were "not-so-good," and some days were a combination of the two. There were days that Bee enjoyed mental clarity, emotional stability, and mounting physical strength. There were also days that her mind seemed a little "fuzzy," her emotions appeared to be on edge, and she would fight against fatigue. Spiritually, she stayed as solid as a rock. Her faith in God remained strong. Her commitment to

God's love was unshakeable.

By this time in our cancer adventure, my ministry had expanded beyond the church. Early in our confrontation with the disease, Bee and I had discussed various contingency plans should something "happen" to her. One option that came to mind was the possibility of becoming a chaplain for a local hospice. Bee and I had both served as volunteers for The Hospice of East Texas in Tyler. We had been honored to visit with patients and offer them support as they had journeyed to the end of life. We had taken the time to listen as family members swapped stories and shared memories. Also, I had been involved with helping children who had experienced loss and who were going through the grieving process. When Bee was first diagnosed with breast cancer, I was volunteering for the bereavement department, making follow-up support calls to families and caregivers. I deemed it a privilege to talk with people whose hearts were heavy and remind them they were not alone.

For years I had thought and prayed about ministering as a hospice chaplain, but I had not taken the time necessary to pursue the training it would require. Now, with Bee facing an uncertain future, I felt it was time to test the waters and see what the Lord might have in store. I applied for and was accepted into the Clinical Pastoral Education (CPE) program at Trinity Mother Frances Hospital in Tyler. The year-long residency is offered to ministers who have a heart-felt desire to serve as chaplains in a clinical setting. The application process was comprehensive and the study was intense, combining hours of pastoral education/instruction and spiritual self-reflection/introspection, along with personal ministry to patients, their families, their friends, and hospital staff on a daily basis (including 24-hour call rotations). The year 2010-2011 would prove to be the most influential, life-changing year I had ever experienced, and CPE would play a major role.

Even though I became involved with hospital ministry, life for Bee and me continued to progress at a snail's pace. The days became weeks, somehow. The weeks became months, somehow. Gradually, we found ourselves finding some sense of normalcy returning to our lives. Only this "normal" was not the same "normal" as what we had been used to. Each day ended with an **aftertaste** that was both unmistakable and hard to describe. Bee's hair began to grow back, but instead of the fine, auburn/brown hair that she had before chemo, this hair was a coarse mixture of black and grey. She had the same wonderful smile, but her eyes didn't have the same twinkle as before. Her desire to work for God and to be a blessing to others remained fervent, but her physical strength rarely allowed her to accomplish all that was in her heart. Eventually she went back to work, but her job was different. Instead of crisscrossing East Texas visiting patients in their homes, she worked in the office with a computer, reviewing charts and "coding." I remained busy in ministry, but it had become necessary for me to resign my pastorate and give full attention to my work at the hospital. The more time I spent at the hospital, the more I enjoyed the change in ministry focus, and I began to think about my options after the CPE residency was finished. Would I return to pastoring or would I find an opportunity to work as a hospice chaplain?

Little-by-little, step-by-step, breath-by-breath, Bee and I saw that life was changing for the two of us. The pressure of cancer and all that goes with it began to slowly subside. We were almost to the point of getting used to the **aftertaste**. We began to breathe deeply again… cautiously. We began to let ourselves think about the future again… guardedly. Skies that had been dominated by the heavy, dark, grey clouds of disease, were beginning to lighten and show hopeful signs of soon-to-come healthy sunshine. Bee was recovering, and I was recovering with her. Life was different, but it wasn't *too* bad, not *too* bad at all.

COGITATION:

Every day is a special gift. Unwrap it with enthusiasm and care. Embrace it with gratitude and thankfulness. Make memories that will be cherished... Always.

Deuteronomy 29:29 says, "The secret things belong unto the Lord our God..." The word, "secret" comes from the Hebrew meaning of "hidden" or "covered." If something is hidden or covered, it doesn't mean that it does not exist; it simply means that whatever "it" is, it is not easily seen and/or recognized.

These words became alive to me one night during this time of Bee's recovery. I was unable to sleep. My mind was wandering. I was thinking about the months of sickness and misery that she and I had been through. I was wondering about what the future would hold. I was contemplating the dips, and curves, and potholes of life. My head was filled with questions, most of which had no answer. When would the struggle be over? What would life look like after this trial? Would I be ministering? Would I be working? What would happen to Bee? Why had all this happened to us?

It was about 2:00 o'clock in the wee hours of the morning when I finally slipped off the bed and out the back door of the house. The night was dark. The air was warm. The sky was clear. The stars were shimmering. A gentle breeze softly touched shadowy needles of the pine trees, and the ground was covered in a light blanket of dew. I walked to a patio/deck where we had some lawn chairs arranged and sat down in silence.

For some time, I sat there, quiet and alone. Suddenly, my eye caught sight of a falling star. A long, thin trail of fire lit up the night as it quickly made its way across the sky. I blinked and it vanished. But, other stars, thousands, millions of other stars, still filled the heavens above the little wooden deck where I was. I continued to look up at the tiny little spots of light for some time, mesmerized by their beauty and vast numbers. Then something very special happened. I heard with my heart the Lord, as He asked me a question: *"How many stars are there?"* "I don't know" was my reply. *"Good answer,"* He said, *"however, just because you don't know how many stars there are, doesn't mean that I don't know how many there are. Just because you don't know the answer to a question, doesn't mean there is no answer to that question. When you don't know... the correct response for you is... 'I don't know.'"*

As I rehearsed the words that had been dropped into my heart by *"divine conversation,"* I was filled with a fresh feeling of peace. The scenarios that had filled my mind earlier began to fade away. I was reminded that I was not required to have all of the answers to all of life's questions. A weight was lifted from my chest. A burden was taken off my shoulders. At that moment, on that deck, in a season of prayerful contemplation, the Lord had spoken a truth into my life, i.e., **The secret things belong to Him. He knows those things that are hidden to me. He is aware of all that is covered. He alone is All Knowing. My role is to trust Him. My challenge is to allow Him to work His will in my life. My desire must be to love Him deeply and to keep my faith firmly anchored to all that He is.**

A GRIEF THOUGHT:

As I have mentioned earlier, questions are often a part of the grieving process. Especially if the death is sudden and/

or traumatic, asking questions in order to gain a better understanding of the event is crucial. Information, knowledge, and corroboration of facts associated with the death can often give the person who is grieving a much-needed feeling of control and stability. Inquiry can help make "sense" out of what otherwise might seem to be a "senseless" loss of life. For others, who experience a lengthy illness and death, the questioning process may begin even before the loss occurs. Reasoning, rationalizing, and second-guessing decisions are common pieces of the grief puzzle.

Questions provide pathways for us to explore loss in our lives. You may not find an answer to every question that you ask, but in giving yourself permission to ask the question, ponder the possibilities, and review the story, you find yourself in a different place than if you simply say, "I shouldn't ever question." It is natural to ask, "Why?" It is normal to think, "What If?" It is not unusual to wonder to yourself, "Who am I?" Many people think to themselves, "How will I be able to live without____?" or "What am I going to do now?"

We live in an information-rich world. We practically drip with technology. We are accustomed to finding answers to all sorts of questions with little-to-no effort. With a few strokes of the keyboard, a move of the mouse, or maybe by saying "Hey____," we find ourselves inundated with definitions, explanations, expert opinions, images, book suggestions, and videos on the subject. However, when it comes to death and grief (*Life*) we are sometimes reminded that not all questions have short, easy-to-understand answers. There are still situations, circumstances, and events that refuse to yield to logic. There are instances, even today, when the correct answer is... "I Don't Know" ... and that is okay.

CHAPTER 7

ALWAYS COME TO A COMPLETE STOP BEFORE SHIFTING INTO REVERSE

A New Diagnosis

Life for Bee and the family appeared to be moving forward at a semi-steady pace, although in a new and different direction. Daily we were putting some distance between us and the dark, murky, swamp waters of disease that we had recently slogged through. Bee was busy back at work, sharing her knowledge and experience with her co-workers. I was busy with chaplain ministry at the hospital. Our son Ben was busy working as a Band Director for Henderson ISD, and our daughter Ruth was busy finishing her degree at Baylor.

There were evenings when Bee would come home very, very tired. She would tell me, "Something is just not quite right, but I can't seem to put my finger on what it is." We would continue to talk about her day, and eventually we would agree that it was going to take more time to get back to operating at 100%. She was probably still adjusting. She was probably trying to do too much too soon. She was probably expecting too much from herself. That is what we would say out loud, however, down deep I believe we both knew that something really was "not-quite-right"; we just didn't know what.

The holidays came and went with a blur ,and the new year began with very little fanfare. Bee kept working. I kept working. Soon enough, the bleakness of winter began to fade and, in its place, the colorful blooms of spring appeared. One of the highlights of an East Texas spring is watching the snow-white flower of the dogwood tree as it floats and bends with the breeze. About 45 miles from where we lived, in the little city of Palestine, there is a wonderful drive-through park hewn out of the East Texas woods that gives special attention to the dogwood tree. One Saturday morning in March, Bee and I decided that it would be a great spot to visit. We could enjoy the trip there and take a well-deserved "deep breath" once we got there. Along the way we could soak up some of the warm spring sunshine and take in the beauty of nature.

Months earlier, after Bee had "graduated" from chemo treatments, to celebrate the achievement Ben had made arrangements for the two of us to take a motorcycle operations course. Upon passing the course, it became clear that we had acquired a fairly useless skill unless we actually owned a motorcycle. So, I bought a *Victory "8" ball* for myself and a *Suzuki* for Bee. We enjoyed riding together along the backroads on the weekends when the weather was good, and it was on these motorcycles that we set out to explore the dogwood trees.

The day was gorgeous. The spring air smelled fresh and sweet. The sun was warm but not hot. The clouds were high and wispy. We rode down the country highway happy to be alive, well and able to enjoy all the sights, sounds, and smells along the way. We arrived at the Davey Dogwood Park in Palestine, Texas, just a little before noon. We rode our motorcycles slowly up and down the hills within the park boundaries, thrilled by the display of dogwood blossoms that filled the forest in every direction. Eventually it came time to park our motorcycles and pull out the picnic. As we were getting off our bikes, I noticed that Bee seemed to be just a bit unsteady. I went to where she stood and helped remove her helmet and gloves. With her helmet off, I could see that her face was pale and her neck was flushed. She was perspiring and shaking ever-so-slightly. I was concerned about her. Not surprisingly, she was concerned about me being concerned about her.

Bee spread the picnic lunch out on the table and we both tried to rest and relax for a while. I was beginning to think that the trip had been too much for her, and I was worried that she might not feel strong enough to make the ride back home. We didn't say much as we sat there; we just munched on our meal, held hands in the sunshine, and quietly thought about life and all the "stuff" that goes with it.

Bee finally broke the silence and admitted that she was not feeling well and suggested we begin our journey back to the house. We quickly packed away the picnic provisions and prepared to leave. As we were getting on our bikes, she told me that she wanted to take the "scenic loop" on the way out of the park. With our gear on and motorcycles cranked we pulled away from the pavilion and made our way toward the little scenic loop detour. Bee was riding ahead of me and as we went around the first corner, I could tell that she seemed a bit "wobbly." I continued to keep an eye on her as we slowly made our way along the narrow park road, riding among the dainty dogwood trees. And then it happened. We came to a sharp, hairpin uphill turn. I could tell by the sound of her motor and the lean in her body that she was not going to make it. I watched in helpless horror as the motorcycle lunged off the road and slid down the side of the hill with Bee pinned underneath!

By the time I could get stopped and go down the hill, Bee was struggling to get out from under her bike. It was heavy and she was exhausted. The pine needles and leaves of the forest floor had cushioned her fall, but the motorcycle had been pretty well bent and busted up by the accident. Bee and I tried to get the machine to the road where I could assess the damage and try to figure out how to get home. In the process Bee stumbled and fell two more times, her energy non-existent. Muted waves of fear and panic pulsed through my body as I tried to form an idea of what to do. Bee was confused, embarrassed, shaken, scared, and scarred. She was also determined to get back on that motorcycle and get home.

Finally, a Good Samaritan happened by, saw our situation, and offered to help. Once we got the motorcycle back on the pavement, I could tell that a tail-light was broken, a fender bent, the handlebars were crooked, and the head-light was hanging limp. Using the few simple tools that I had with me, I was able to straighten the fender, adjust the handlebars (some), re-position the head-light (a little), and taped up the tail-light. The Suzuki didn't look too good, but it would make the trip home. The question was, would Bee? She had been shaking like a leaf with fatigue, and it was apparent that the incident had left a deep impression on her. However, after a short rest, she was able to gather herself enough to get back on the motorcycle and start home.

I will never forget that ride home. It seemed to take forever. I was riding closely behind Bee, the whole way feeling as though my stomach were in my mouth. Every so often I would notice her bike wiggle slightly, and I would feel a fresh wave of panic. With each oncoming vehicle, I was afraid she would lose control and swerve into its path. I could hear the uncertain sound of her engine as she struggled to maintain a steady grip on the throttle. About half way home the wind whipped the tape on the tail-light loose and I watched as it dangled and flapped with the turbulence.

At last we made it home and after a hot shower, Bee went to bed. That evening, as she drifted off to sleep, it was vaguely apparent that she was not the same woman she was when we had left that morning... not really. The next week we made an appointment with our family doctor. After listening to us tell the tale of our "dogwood adventure," and reviewing Bee's chart, it was decided that a CT scan was in order. The nurse called the hospital and set things up. The next day we found ourselves back in another waiting room, sitting in anticipation of hearing Bee's name called and making a trip to the "back" where another scan would be done.

The scan was done. The images were analyzed and reviewed. The result was... *Cancer* again. The Breast Cancer had metastasized and three tumors had formed on Bee's brain.

Without noticeable warning, we experienced a gut-wrenching, heart-pounding change in direction. It was as though we had been driving down the road content with the progress we were making, then suddenly the shift lever had been yanked from my hand and our world slammed into reverse. Common sense says that when you are driving down the highway it is not a good idea to reach down and arbitrarily decide to move the little red arrow from the "D" to the "R." The change causes damage to your vehicle. The engine, the transmission, the brakes, the tires, and who-knows-what-else are all affected in a negative way. Yes, you should always come to a complete stop before shifting into reverse... **We Could Not.**

Behind the "Book-Writing Curtain"

It has been over two months since I have been able to work on this chapter of the book. I knew I needed to finish the project, but I have felt frozen, blocked, blank, intimidated, stuck, unable to go forward. The reason? This is the point in the story where everything in life began to change. Because I know how abrupt and definitive the change was, it is difficult to reflect on some of the events that took place during this time. Although I've shared with many people on many occasions bits and pieces of what took place, the details are still *very impactful and significant when stacked together. **An individual piece of thread weighs very little, and yet many woven together can produce a mighty heavy blanket.** The following is an account of what I did in an effort to get back to writing the story...*

"A penny for your thoughts." It's an expression I have heard all my life. I have never thought that any of my thoughts were ever actually worth a penny, but the expression does have a way of causing us to pause and pay attention to what we are thinking about in that moment we are offered a penny for them. The fact is, when we stop to think about what we are thinking about, it can be very revealing.

For months I put off writing about the events that I have outlined in this chapter. Each time I would think about sitting down and going to work I would find an excuse not to. It didn't take long hours of introspection or self-reflection to realize that at the center of my hesitancy was the memory of the day Bee and I went for that motorcycle ride to the Davey Dogwood Park. My thoughts would always wander back to the wreck on the hairpin turn. The question that I had to find an answer for was, "How am I going to get past this and finish writing the story?"

I decided that I would take a day and return to the place where it all took place. I felt that it was important to intentionally remember all I could about that day. And so, on a warm summer morning I ate a bite of breakfast, drank a cup of coffee, climbed into my pick-up truck, and struck out for the dogwood park where my life was changed forever. All that I took with me was a note pad to write my thoughts on and my memory of that dreadful day in the spring of 2011.

This is what I wrote:

Heading for the dogwood trail. Beginning my trip, I feel my stomach tightening up slightly. My heartrate is faster than normal. I have deliberately chosen not to turn the radio on. No news. No music. No distractions. I want to quietly, privately, and purposefully concentrate on my thoughts and memories. I have a job to do. I have a task to complete. I have a story to tell. My hands are slightly warm. My palms slightly sweaty. My legs feel slightly weak/numb as I drive down the highway.

I look out the window of my truck and see lots of fluffy, puffy clouds. They have high white tops and boast all sorts of billowy shapes. They change with the wind. The clouds are flat and dark grey at the bottom. The more I look, the more the clouds seem to be coming together in the distance. Later there may be rain.

Getting closer now. My focus is on driving. Suddenly a faint, fleeting thought. My mind wanders back to where I am going and why. My mouth waters. My eyes water. I look out the window. Just ahead, a little to my left, and barely above the tree tops, the horizon is filled with clouds. They are forming a solid grey wall now. It's raining in the distance.

I turn off the main road and here I am. Back in the Davey Dogwood Park. Slowly I make my way along the narrow winding road that is lightly covered with leaves and pine straw. With the windows down, I can hear the wind as it wanders among the tree tops. Up and down and around I go, following the little asphalt trail. The route curves among an array of oaks, elms, hickory, pine, and dogwood trees. Here and there I spy patches of green summer grass accented by a stray sun beam that has broken through the forest canopy. A small spring-fed stream seeps out of the hillside and flows lazily over a sandy, iron-ore creek-bottom. Around one more bend, between the hills, I see a small valley where one little creek meets another. There is an open meadow. The local Rotary club has erected a well-kept metal pavilion that stands in the middle of the opening between the hills. It serves as a place to rest, relax, celebrate, and to remember… I pull my pick-up close and pause for a minute or two. It's a beautiful, peaceful place. However, I can't stay here long, because my mind is moving me closer to "Scenic Loop 3." That's where the accident happened. That's where my life began to change.

My pulse quickens as I pull away from the pavilion and head for the entrance to the scenic loop. I make the turn and immediately the one-way road leads me up a steep path that curves along the hillside. At the top of the hill there is a gentle down-grade, followed by another gentle curve. That curve is followed by a hairpin turn to the left that goes back up the hill. This is it.

I find a safe spot to park the truck. I turn off the engine, open the door, and slide out. I walk past the hairpin and up the hill to the place where the motorcycle wreck took place. My muscles strain and pull a bit as I trek up the steep rise. The road seems to flatten out at the exact location where it all took place. I am perplexed. Why right here? As I stand here looking down the hill where Bee and the motorcycle had ended up, I begin to notice a tug/pull on my body. My eyes cannot see it, but my body can definitely feel the force of gravity as it tries to coax me down that same hill. This was the force that had overcome Bee's weakness and had caused her to crash among the leaves and sticks and bushes at the bottom.

I stand here and ponder for a long time. I take slow deep breaths. I make myself remember as much as I can remember. I embrace what happened. Finally, it is time to turn away and go. I think, "What can I leave to make this a special place?" I look in my pick-up for something. I find a shiny new penny. "A penny for your thoughts" goes through my mind. How appropriate. I walk back up the hill and right next to the road where the wreck had happened is a hickory tree. On the side of the tree, facing the road is a new limb that is beginning to form just about eye level. Above the limb, I discover a slight indention in the bark. It is a perfect place... a thoughtful place... to put that penny. I do.

As I walk back down the hill, I notice that there is a slight breeze blowing. It gently rolls a few leaves past my feet. I can't feel it. I stop and turn around. Facing it, I feel refreshed. It is time to leave.

I climb back into my truck and start for the park exit. There are more curves to go around. There are some really steep hills to go up and down. There is more beauty to see. Around one last curve there is an EXIT sign. It isn't long before I turn out of the park and on to the main road. As I pull away, I glance at my rearview mirror, and I take one more look at the place where my life changed.

Driving home, my stomach still lets me know that I'm on a special trip. My thoughts still drift backwards and hover around the events that happened in the spring of 2011. But the sun is out now. The white and grey clouds are still there, only now my eyes are drawn to the brilliant blue sky around them. I have thoughts of the long ride home that Bee and I made years ago. Today, the road is smooth. *I Will Travel On*.

COGITATION:

Memories are powerfully important in grief. We pour from Yesterday, a foundation upon which we build Today, in preparation for something special Tomorrow.

A GRIEF THOUGHT

The grieving process does not eliminate all the pain nor all the memories associated with a loss. However, over time the pain becomes less intense and all consuming. At some point along the grief journey, most people find that their memories begin to bring them a certain amount of comfort. The goal of grief is not to get us to the place that we forget abruptly, but to get us to a place where we can remember gently.

Some people resist grief because they are afraid that they will forget the one they have loved and lost. In their view, the possibility of forgetting is as painful as the loss itself. There are people who feel guilty if they are not constantly thinking about the person in their life who has died. They worry that if they were to smile or laugh, or have a happy thought or a hopeful thought about the future, somehow, they are leaving their loved one behind. Rest assured, you will not forget the one you love. It's okay to move forward and keep them in your heart and mind as you do. You do not have to forget!

On the other hand, there are some who try their best to forget. Memories are painful to them, so they diligently try to remove anything that would serve as a trigger to remember. Some turn to disruptive or deviant behavior in an effort to escape the pain associated with the death. Drugs, alcohol, sex, even excessive work habits, only serve to cover up the feelings, emotions, and memories associated with grief. The pain and awkwardness found in those who survive is caused by the death, and giving yourself permission to remember the one who died is part of the healing process. It has been said that by releasing our pain, we make room for our healing. However, before you can release your pain, you must first be willing to accept it. Memories help us to both hold on and let go.

Memories are a part of who we are. They are a natural part of the grieving process. Often, we spend so much time and energy trying to either remember or trying to forget what happened in our lives yesterday that we miss the wonder of what's happening in our lives today. Perhaps it would be best if we simply gave ourselves permission to remember what we remember and not worry too much about what we forget.

Whenever you plan on taking a road trip, whether it be across the city, or across the country, once you are behind the steering wheel and the engine has been started, the first appropriate step is to check the rearview mirror. It is not a bad idea to be aware of what is behind you, before you focus on what is in front. As you live your life, try not to get so focused on the view through the windshield that you forget to glance out the back window from time to time. It's important to see where you're going, but it's also important to see where you've been.

The day I took the time to go back and embrace the memories of my past was the day that I found the freedom to face my future.

CHAPTER 8

SLOWLY MOVING QUICKLY

The Summer Months

f you were to pick up a Bible and turn to the book of 1 Kings, chapter 17, you would find the record of the first days of public ministry for the prophet of God... **Elijah**. Not much is written about his personal history or "theological" training. All that we know is, he was a Tishbite who had been living in the land of Gilead. Without warning or fanfare, he leaps out of the shadows of obscurity, onto the stage of history, stands firmly in front of King Ahaz, and declares; *"As the Lord God of Israel liveth, before whom I stand, there shall not be dew nor rain these years, but according to my word."*

After he makes this statement, the Lord gives him instruction and a promise... "*Go to the east, and hide yourself by the little brook Cherith that flows into the Jordan river. When you get there, you will find water to drink in case you get thirsty, and I have made arrangements with some of the local birds to bring you something to eat, so that you don't get hungry.*" *(paraphrased)*

And so, it was. Elijah went eastward to hide next to Cherith, where he drank water from the creek and ate what the birds brought him every morning and evening for over a year. It was a place of special provision. However, verse seven says, "*And it came to pass after a while, that the brook dried up, because there had been no rain in the land.*"

Let that statement sink in. "*The brook dried up.*" Think about it... the brook did not dry up overnight. It was a slow process. It is not easy to stay still and/or stay put while watching your only source of water dry up right before your eyes, but Elijah did. Elijah remained obedient to the word of the Lord. He didn't go upstream in search of a better creek or downstream toward a bigger river. He didn't wander off in search of a different breed of birds to bring him food. He didn't begin to set off in search of a more loving and caring God. He did not budge, even though he knew that the babbling brook that had once slaked his thirst was steadily becoming a dry arroyo. Elijah simply committed himself to faithfully trust in God. He knew that the Lord had sent him to be where he was, and that was enough to keep him from leaving on his own. However, what he did not know was, while living in that place of dwindling resources, just down the road in a little town called Zarephath, the Lord was preparing *another place* for him to live that would be *another place* of special provision. It wouldn't be long, and the Lord would send him there.

Understand, the prophet of God was able to stay by the brook as long as he did, not because his faith was in the waters of Cherith, but because his faith was in the God who had led him there. In due time, Elijah was able to walk away from the place of one miracle and move toward the middle of another, because his eyes were focused on the provider, not the provision. Elijah knew that, regardless of the circumstance and/or situation, the Lord was in loving control of his life. The apostle John put it this way, "**God opens things that no man can shut, and He shuts things that no man can open**" **(Revelation 3:7)**. Elijah trusted God enough to let Him do all the opening and shutting. "*...After a while, the brook dried up...*" one miracle was coming to an end; another miracle was just about to begin.

By late spring, Bee and I both began to realize that God was gently closing one door and, at the same time, tenderly opening another. We had a sense that life was about to change for both of us. We were not discouraged, depressed, or defeated. We were walking with God, and He was walking in a direction that we had hoped to avoid. But still we pressed forward by faith. During the summer months, everything in my world seemed to… *slowly move quickly.*

Soon after detecting the brain tumors, Bee started radiation treatment in an effort to slow the growth of the cancer. The idea was for her to undergo ten rounds of radiation and then the doctors would assess her condition to determine the most advisable plan of care going forward. It didn't take but a few trips to the "radiation room" for Bee to lose what little strength she had regained in the months after her chemo regimen. She quickly became weak, frail, unsteady, and somewhat confused. After five or six treatments she was forced to take a break, and the doctor took a look at the scans to try to get a feel for how the tumors were reacting. The news was not good. Three tumors were not responding to the radiation. We decided to press on, but after two more treatments, it was clear that Bee's remaining strength was spent. Her body was worn to a frazzle, and the tumors were showing no signs of shrinking.

The doctor invited Bee and myself into her office to discuss the situation. She looked across her desk, leaned forward in her chair, and spoke in a soft tone words of knowledge and compassion. Radiation was not working. The cancer was not responding. There were two basic options open to us: 1. Brain surgery 2. Hospice care.

Option 1 would be very risky considering Bee's fragile condition, along with the location and depth of the tumors. Successful removal of the cancer was a long shot. The percentages were high that if Bee were to survive the surgery, her motor skills and cognition would be severely affected. Most likely she would live the rest of her days in a "vegetative "state. She would need to be moved into a nursing facility, and she would be confined to the bed, dependent on staff for complete 24-hour care. Given the aggressive nature of the cancer, Bee was given no more than six months to live.

I looked at Bee; she looked at me, and we held hands. Warm tears began to well up in our eyes and silently run down our cheeks. My stomach tightened. My knees went weak. My heart began to pound. Life had brought us to a crossroads that we had discussed off and on for over thirty years. We had often agreed that at the end of life, should we be blessed with the opportunity to choose, we would rather die with dignity than have our days extended solely dependent on medical manipulation, machinery, or experimentation. It did not take long for us to decide… Bee chose option 2, hospice care.

As we told the doctor that Bee wished to be referred to hospice, it wasn't helplessness or hopelessness that we felt, but rather a deep sense of love and peace. *We both knew that the time had come for us to change our focus from trying to find a cure for a dreadful disease, to providing comfort and care for my wonderful wife.*

On July 5, 2011, a referral was sent to The Hospice of East Texas and a request was made for a nurse to come to our house to do an initial evaluation/assessment of Bee's condition. The goal from the beginning was to keep Bee as pain free and comfortable as possible, for as long as possible. The support was immediate, comprehensive, and genuine. In a very short time, a schedule was established that included regular visits from the hospice doctor, the nurse, the CNA, the social worker, and the chaplain. A hospice volunteer was made available as well.

As I mentioned earlier, end-of-life care was not

a new concept to either of us. Bee and I had served as hospice volunteers for many years. The Hospice of East Texas had by this time offered me a job as Bereavement Coordinator. Both of us had walked with people who had taken the journey that we were now about to begin. We had been with many people who had been terminally ill, but we soon discovered that... *it's different when it's you.*

As the caring and efficient staff of The Hospice of East Texas began to share their skills with us, I found myself feeling free to be something other than Bee's caregiver. I could embrace the role of Bee's husband, best friend, and soulmate again. I could focus my love on my wife without trying to assess her need or manage her pain. She and I could sit and reminisce about the past, or talk about what life would be like in the future, without having to deal with dark clouds of question and concern. The course was set. The Lord was in total control. Our hands were off the steering wheel. It was very comforting and quite liberating for both of us.

If there had been any doubt about our decision to go onto hospice service, it would have vanished within a two-week period. By that time, it was evident that the cancer was growing; Bee's pain was increasing, her cognition was decreasing, and she was becoming more and more restless, agitated, confused, and hard to manage. She was sick! It wasn't long before her speech was affected, as well as her mobility. When she tried to stand, she was weak and unsteady. When she tried to walk, she was prone to fall. When she fell, it was difficult to get her back up. The tumors continued to grow and press on the nerves deep within her brain, which caused her to be combative, uncooperative, and hard to console at times.

Weeks went by, and even with exceptional care and symptom management, Bee's condition continued to decline. Life began to morph into something totally different than anything I had experienced before. I found myself facing a new flood of feelings and a new depth of emotion. Everything seemed to be all mixed up and mixed together. I tried to sort things out in my head, but the harder I tried, the more frustrated I felt. It was like reaching into a huge bowl of spaghetti and trying to straighten out individual pieces of pasta one at a time… tediously difficult!

During this time, "Time" took on a whole new meaning. Day and night became elongated, strangely-stretched-out-of-shape concepts. In some ways, I felt like time was barely dragging by, as if an invisible ball and chain were attached to the grandfather clock in the living room. On those days, life was like pulling taffy in slow motion.

Whenever I tried to adjust to this "slow go," without warning, time would seem to speed up and life would begin to spin at break-neck speed. Everything in my world would swish by in a blur and leave me feeling dizzy. There were times when I felt as if I were in a dream and I was trying to run... fast... but the harder I tried to run fast, the slower I got. At other times I would try to slow down, but the more I applied the brakes, the faster I would find myself racing forward. **UGH!**

As the hot, muggy days of summer continued to add up, I was doing my best to finish the chaplain residency at the hospital that I had started the previous year. Ministry to patients, their families, and staff, became more of a challenge, knowing that my wife was locked in a life and death struggle with cancer. As I walked the halls and made my visits, my stomach usually felt as if I had swallowed a brick. My mind constantly drifted toward thoughts of home and the love of my life: Bee. However, we were blessed with a host of wonderful friends and loving family who helped take care of her on those long days I had to spend away, and in the end, I was able to complete my

CPE training.

When I was able to be at home with Bee, the days were long, but the nights were longer. It would take a while, but eventually she would get easy enough to fall asleep. While she slept, I would lie awake listening to her breathe and watching for her to move ever-so-slightly. I wondered what would happen should she die in her sleep in the bed next to me. I tried to imagine how I would react. I thought about Ben and Ruth. I thought about love. I thought about the past. I thought about the future. Warm tears would fill my eyes. Hard lumps would fill my throat. My spine would tingle.

In the darkness, I questioned decisions that had been made, and then questioned them again, and then again. I believed that Bee and I had done all that we had known to do, and I had no regrets, but still, I wrestled with uncertainty. I knew that one day Bee would be gone, and then what? I was doing my best to prepare, but it was like getting ready for a major hurricane. I knew that it was coming; I knew that it would be devastating, and I knew that I would face a season of clean-up and recovery afterward. But, how would I make it through the storm once it hit? … that remained a question. Days were long. Nights were longer.

COGITATION:

The Lord is Mighty, even at Midnight! David wrote, "The Lord will command his lovingkindness, in the day time, and in the night his song shall be with me..." (Psalm 42:8)

A GRIEF THOUGHT

When combining the many and varied effects of grief, with the often-overwhelming responsibilities of caregiving, the **caregiver** is often lost in the shuffle. With this in mind it is absolutely crucial for the one who is giving care to take care of themselves! Think about it, before you can give anything, you must have something to give. Or, said another way, once what you have has been given, you no longer have what you need/desire to give. **Caregiver, Take Care!**

Caregivers are people who give care to others, but it's more than a simple description of what they do. It is a complex definition of who they are. I believe a true caregiver is more than someone who just "does" because it has to be done; a true caregiver "does" because their heart is involved in the process of doing. They give of themselves physically, mentally, emotionally, socially, and spiritually. For them, caregiving can be defined as: a combination of effort and energy held together by love and devotion.

With so much going out, it is highly important to make sure that you don't run out. If you do run out or run low on what fuels you, it's also important that you know where to go for a refill. Be encouraged to find out/remember what "fills" you with energy, enthusiasm, motivation, joy, peace, hope, faith, etc. ***Taking time to refuel is never wasted time.***

Caution... the tank does not receive more gas just because you know where the gas station is. Driving by the pump and looking at the hose hanging provides very little real help down the road. You have to be deliberate in the refueling process. *(It doesn't have to take long, but it is necessary if you want to keep going.)*

Let me briefly remind you of the refueling process… *First,* glance at the gauge on a regular basis and pay attention to the "needle." *Next,* evaluate/assess the situation. Think about how much fuel you have. Think about where you are and where you want/need to be along the journey. Think about what options and opportunities for refueling present themselves. When you get a chance to get more fuel, take advantage of it, even if it means little more than topping off your tank. You never know how far you may have to go before you get another crack at it. Think… **some is always better than none.** Whenever you have a moment… grab it! Take a deep breath, step on the brake, turn the steering wheel, pull off the highway and into the filling station. Once you come to a complete stop, turn off the engine, and focus on the refueling process.

When it comes to the caregiver refueling process, here are some basics:

1. Learn how to ask for and to accept help. ("Lone Rangers" get really lonely and wear out really quickly.)

2. Coordinate care with other family, friends, and/or caregivers if possible. Develop a plan.

3. Create a support network that covers physical, emotional, mental, social, and spiritual needs. If you have a phone… use it. If you have a computer… use it. If you know how to send smoke signals… do it!

4. Identify available resources specific to your situation and learn from information. Knowledge leads to confidence, and confidence leads to empowerment.

5. Give yourself permission to feel feelings and experience emotions. It requires a tremendous amount of energy to remain stiff and stoic

when everything in you wants to feel and emote.

Here it is… Caregivers are people who are responsible for someone else's care and who give that care out of a loving heart. When added together, grief and responsibility present a heavy weight to carry from day to day. If you want to continue giving care, you must continually take care of yourself. *Remember: if you don't have it, you can't give it.* Choose to do what you need to do in order to refuel along this care-giving journey. **Caregiver, Take Care!**

COGITATION

If you spread the peanut butter too thin, you'll begin to rip the bread.

CHAPTER 9

LIFE... LOVE... LONELINESS

The Loss

The year was 1977. Sister Tucker was a dear "80-something"-year-old African-American woman who was a double-amputee, bed-bound patient in Melrose Nursing Home in Tyler. She was my friend. I was a 17-year-old "preacher boy" who spent most of my Friday evenings ministering to the residents at Melrose. Every week, I would go to visit Sis. Tucker, and every week I would begin my visit by asking the same question, "Sis. Tucker, how are you today?" Every time I asked that question, I would get the same response. Sis. Tucker would raise her frail little arms toward heaven, look at me with a far-away tear in her eye, and say, "I've got my hands in God's hands, and I'm gonna keep on, keepin' on!" I was blessed by what she said, and how she said it, every time. Over the years, her words of faith have echoed through my life again and again… "I've got my hands in God's hands, and I'm gonna keep on keepin' on!"

In the summer of 2011, the weeks were slipping by, and Bee's condition was getting more intense. Her pain was extreme. Her cognition was growing more limited. Her strength was sporadic and came in short, syncopated spurts. Friends and family were rallying around us with support. At the hospital, my chaplain friends were giving me tremendous, unselfish, whole-hearted help, as I worked on finishing my year of residency. The staff of The Hospice of East Texas were phenomenal in everything they were doing for Bee and the family. Still, it felt like I had climbed up and out of a narrow muddy trench by way of an unsteady wooden ladder and was now running through a smoky haze toward an unseen enemy who was determined to teach me a new definition of death.

There were moments of fear and dread. There were times of confusion and anxiety. There were days when my thoughts were consumed with the fight. However, even though I *felt* like I was on a battlefield, beneath my feelings, my *faith* remained firm. *I knew* that no matter what, when, or how in the end, there would be **Peace,** because *I knew* the outcome was not up to the enemy, but rather, *The Lord.* I was committed to *keeping my hands in God's hands.* I was determined to *keep on, keepin' on!*

Not too many days had been marked off the month of August before Bee had to be transferred to The Hospice of East Texas' inpatient facility, "Home Place," for symptom management. Highly-trained, skilled and professional doctors, nurses, and CNAs worked tirelessly trying to get Bee's pain and agitation regulated. It proved to be a daily challenge as the brain tumors continued to grow. Her body would respond to a medication regimen for maybe 12 or 18 or 24 hours, and then things would quickly spiral out-of-control and a new protocol would have to be determined. When we had first arrived at Home Place, we had planned on getting Bee's pain managed and then, after a few days, going back home more settled. As it turns out, days turned into weeks, and nothing happened the way we had planned.

Finally, early on Sunday morning September 4, 2011, after weeks of extensive, intensive, and

extraordinary, compassionate care, Bee took one...
last... short... shallow breath. It was the end of her
two-year struggle with an awful earthly disease and
the beginning of eternal freedom from pain, sorrow,
and darkness of night. I sat quietly beside her bed as
her body gently relaxed, and she settled into rest. I was
shaken ever-so-slightly by the stillness of the moment.
An amazing, "almost-heard" silence filled the room.
Bee had gone. I was left. Bee had died. I was alive.

It wasn't long before I began to feel the heavy
weight of **Life, Love,** and **Loneliness,** as my mind and
my heart were filled by a flood of thoughts, feelings,
and emotions. My chaplain training and knowledge
of bereavement told me that I was "normal." I was
grieving. I would be okay. My broken heart told me
that I was "leaving" and "arriving" at the same time.
I was both "walking out" and "walking in" like I had
stumbled into an on-going episode of "*The Twilight
Zone.*" It might have been normal, but at the time, I
wished for some sort of "*emotional remote control*" that
would give me the ability to rewind life and re-live a
more-fun moment. Or, maybe I could find a way to
fast-forward past this particularly unpleasant part and
view a scene that contained less stress. If only there
were a button to push that would cause life to pause,

give me a chance to catch my breath, and get my bearings... There was no remote control... There were no buttons. Regardless... I had put *my hands in God's hands*, and I was going to *keep on, keepin' on.*

Memories of our **life** together and our **love** for each other came barreling into my brain. I remembered the first time I saw Bee. I remembered our first date. I remembered the first coconut pie she baked me. The funny little apartment we called our first home. The miracle surrounding the birth of Ben. The second miracle involving the birth of Ruth. The hundreds of songs she had played on the piano and that I had sung as she played. The countless hours she sat on the pew listening to me preach. All the babies she had taken care of in church nurseries over the years. The patients she had touched with her skill. The friends she had made, and the people she had impressed with her honesty and integrity. Trips we had taken together. Trials we had faced. Joys we had shared. Over thirty years of life and love came rushing in. I was overwhelmed by the experienced. I was comforted by the experience. It made my "tummy" feel warm and my heart beat with a deep calm. I was sorrowful for the loss, but I was thankful for the **life** we had lived and the **love** we had shared. A solid sense of faith gripped my spirit.

My emotions, like my memories, were a motley mixture, and they kept rolling in like ocean waves onto a rocky shore. Sadness, fear, anxiety, relief, guilt, confusion, confidence, depression, excitement, and so much more. It was a big, mixed-up mess. I couldn't figure out how I was "supposed" to feel. I didn't know which feelings were "appropriate." However, I did know the most intense emotion that I felt was *loneliness*. But *this* loneliness was unlike any loneliness I had known before. This was a *"bottomless loneliness,"* dark and deep, without walls or ceiling to give it definition and without a floor for foundation. This loneliness would be consuming later on, but for the moment, it was only one of many feelings that were vying for my attention.

The hands on the clock did not stop. Time continued to "tick" by. Phone calls were made to family and friends. News of Bee's death began to spread rapidly. Eventually, it was time to leave the hospice room and go home. Clothes were gathered up and put in a plastic bag. Pictures and little "what-nots" that had been brought in were collected and packed away in a small suitcase. Sacks of snacks and baskets of fruit that had been given to us were shared with other hospice families that we had met during Bee's stay at Home Place. The funeral home had come, and Bee's body had been reverently removed. Heartfelt hugs of gratitude were given to staff.

I was in a weird-sort-of-daze, and my legs felt like lead, as I began to make my way out the front doors of Home Place. However, as I slowly walked across the parking lot, I began to notice the freshness of the early morning air as it gently touched my tear-stained cheeks. I got to my pick-up, reached for the door handle, and just before getting in, I glanced up at the September sky. The clouds were just beginning to reflect the rays of the new-day sun. Beyond the clouds… a beautiful blue. I took a long, deep breath on purpose. The "weird-sort-of-daze" began to melt away. Climbing into my truck, I whispered a prayer of thanksgiving and praise for the Lord's faithfulness.

As I drove down the road, I wondered about what the future would look like. I tried to imagine what twists and turns my **life** would take in the days, weeks, and months ahead. I thought about how wonderful it was to have lived deeply in **love**. I pondered about how powerful love is and how strong it becomes when shared with someone special. **Life** and **Love**: I continued to reflect on these things, as well as who knows how many more things, for the duration of the drive.

It didn't take more than 30 or 40 minutes before I made the last turn and went up the last hill that led to my house. When I got there, I pulled into the driveway, parked in the garage, and entered through the back door as usual. Except, this day was not usual. The air was thick with silence as I walked into the kitchen and tossed my keys onto the counter. I took a few more steps toward the living room, leaned against the wall, and looked out the window at the distant horizon. My chest felt heavy. My legs were weak. My lips quivered. My heart was pounding. The blood was rushing through my veins. I was both vaguely and acutely aware that my life really had changed forever. The **"bottomless loneliness"** that I had felt earlier that morning was back (and somehow, I understood that it was going to be with me for some time). What I did not understand was the number of unexpected ways loneliness can affect your life. I was in for an education, but *I had my hands in God's hands,* and I was going to *keep on, keepin' on.*

The rest of that day was a blur. Friends, family, church folk, and members of the neighborhood called or came by to share their heart-felt condolences and offer their assistance. People from all over East Texas began to show up at my front door with food. This was the first day of what went on for weeks. I was humbled by the outpouring of love. I was also a bit embarrassed by all the attention. I would much rather have been on the giving end than on the receiving end. Nevertheless, I understood the importance of allowing others the opportunity to do nice things for me during such a special time of life. It was all a part of the grieving/healing process for them, as well as for myself.

The following day was filled with *"making arrangements,"* which involved making decisions, which meant answering questions. Things like: Where would the funeral service take place? What church would be large enough to host the expected number of people? Would there be food for the family, and if so, who would cook it, serve it, and clean up after it was eaten? Would we have... what we call in East Texas... a "Visitation" the evening before the funeral? If so, then when, and where, and for how long? There were questions regarding the obituary information, the number of death certificates needed, which cemetery we wanted to use, what kind of vault would be most appropriate, and which casket should we choose. The questions just kept coming, each one demanding an answer to be given; each one requiring a decision to be made. I embraced the opportunity to be busy, but discovered by the end of the day that "making arrangements" was exhausting!

The day of the funeral was one of the strangest days of my life. After years of being the minister, orchestrating the funeral service, and looking out for the needs of grieving people, I was the one grieving. At lunch, I had to make a conscious effort to sit still and let someone else wait on me, instead of the other way around. I had to be pro-active in **not** taking a leading role in the "order of service." Before the service, it felt weird waiting with the family to be escorted into the church instead of being at the front door shaking hands with the people as they arrived. It was awkward sitting on the pew, surrounded by family, looking up at the pulpit and listening to another preacher give the eulogy. Perhaps the most unusual thing about the events of that day was the realization that this funeral was not for a stranger, friend, or some distant relation. This was Bee's funeral. The picture on the program was Bee's. At the cemetery, the gravesite was prepared for Bee. When I walked away from the grave that day, Bee's body stayed.

After all of the goodbyes had been said, final farewells had been made, and last, long hugs had been given, I slowly walked out of the cemetery. Once again,

I got into my pick-up truck and headed toward home. When I arrived, I was alone. The sun was setting, and the living room was filled with evening shadows as I sat in my chair and re-played the events of that strange day over in my mind. At some point, I picked up a stack of sympathy cards that people had brought to the funeral and began to thumb through them. One in particular caught my eye. It was from Bee's mother. On the inside was a hand-written note thanking me for loving and caring for her daughter for thirty years! *That was it;* when I read those words, the "flood-gates" opened, and I cried... I cried for a *long* time. I was desperately sad and bone tired. I felt like I had been split in two, and everything inside me had been exposed to a cold north wind.

I had no doubt that I was grieving in a "different gear" now that Bee had died. I realized that I would be mourning the loss of my wife for some time to come. I understood that there would be some fairly good days and some really bad days ahead. I knew that in the future there would be crazy busy days to get through and very long nights to endure. But I also knew that in the end, I was going to be alright because I was still committed to *keeping my hands in God's hands;* I was determined to *keep on, keepin' on.*

COGITATION

"Rejoice not against me, O my enemy: when I fall, I shall arise; when I sit in darkness, the Lord shall be a light unto me!" (Micah 7:8)

A GRIEF THOUGHT

It's not original, but the best definition I have for grief is: ***Grief Is Love.*** It is our love extended. Just because someone is no longer with us physically does not mean that we stop loving them. Our Love continues. It is different (because everything is different), but it is love nonetheless. I like to describe the thought in terms of a stringed musical instrument, a violin, or a guitar perhaps. Think of the strings as heart strings. Those strings stay attached to the one you love, and they are there to remind you of that love. You might be having an "okay" day, when out-of-the-blue, you hear a song on the radio, smell a familiar smell, glance in a certain direction, or have a random thought pass through your mind. Before you know it, your stomach is in a knot, or your knees have turned to steamed dumplings, or your throat tightens, and your eyes water. What has happened? What is wrong? You are **not** going crazy; your heart string has been "plucked." You are feeling the vibration of those heart strings. You are being reminded of that special someone and how their life touched your life. Recognize the grief; *Embrace Your Love!*

COGITATION

*"…Be strong and of a good courage;
be not afraid, neither be dismayed:
for the Lord thy God is with thee
whithersoever thou goest." (Joshua 1:9)*

*"My God shall supply all your need according
to his riches in glory." (Philippians 4:19)*

REFLECTION:

The Light in Between

Where do I go from here? How can I make it through the days, weeks, months, and years ahead? What can I do to get past all of the "stuff" that stands in my way?

Have you ever found yourself asking these kinds of questions? Life is full of all sorts of obstacles and obstructions, roadblocks and detours. Often, we get "blocked" from making forward progress by circumstances and situations beyond our control. However, sometimes we get stuck in the same place because our focus is only on those things that divert our attention and hinder our movement.

Have you ever wondered what would happen if we spent as much time looking past the obstacles as we do looking at them? Years ago, I was sitting on my front porch taking in the sights and smells of a lazy summer day just after an afternoon rain shower. The sun was setting in the west; the air was warm and fresh, and tiny droplets of fresh rain water glistened. Across the street there was a thick stand of young sweetgum trees. The green leaves were finely laced together to form a seemingly solid wall that swayed ever so gently in the evening breeze. The scene was beautiful and peaceful.

As I sat in my rocking chair, I took a slow, deep breath in and just as slowly let it out. For some inexplicable reason, the moment felt special. And then I noticed a pair of red birds frolicking in the afore-mentioned foliage. I watched them chase each other in the dense growth. A hop here, a jump there, a flutter of wings, and then off they went flying so fast it was hard to keep my eyes from crossing. It was at this point it occurred to me; I have never seen a bird run into a tree. They fly in and out among limbs, sticks, leaves, pine needles, brambles, branches, and such all day long and not once have I ever seen a bird bounce off any of them. I asked the question,

"Why?" The answer is (in my humble opinion) because they do not focus on the obstacles as they fly; they look for the light in between. The leaves and limbs and other "stuff" that seem to form such a solid barrier to us are, for them, little more than convenient places to rest from time to time.

Maybe we can learn from the birds. Maybe, just maybe, we could spend a little less time looking at the obstacles in our path and a little more time looking past them. Keep in mind; life is always going to include "stuff," but we don't have to be blocked by the "stuff" when we remember to look for the light in between.

CHAPTER 10

THE RIVER STILL FLOWS...

The Future

A few days after Bee's funeral, I found myself sitting in my office staring out the window. It was early in the morning, and the sun was just beginning to shine on the pine trees across the parking lot. I watched as rough brown branches, festooned with long green needles, gently swayed in the wind. Sunshine and shadows danced together on the ground beneath the pine canopy. My window was not open, but in my mind, I could hear the soft swishing sound the wind was making in the tops of those trees. I could imagine the smell of the pine straw that covered the ground. I could envision the pine cones as they dropped from the trees without warning and hear the little "cracking" kind of sound they made when they landed. In one tree a blue jay was jumping from one limb to another, fluffing his feathers with each new perch. In another tree, a squirrel was shaking its tail and chattering "squirrel chatter." I pondered the world just outside my window, and thought: *There is Life yet to be Lived... The River Still Flows.*

I was sad. I was lonely. I was intimidated by feelings of uncertainty. However, I was also excited about what my world would look like in the "tomorrows" that lay on the horizon. I understood that there was work to be done. There were things to do that only I could do. There were people who loved me and who wanted me to love them in return. There were people who needed me. My kids needed their father's love, advice, and support. My co-workers at Hospice needed to hear my ideas on how to encourage patients who were struggling with life-limiting diagnoses. They wanted to know my recommendations for their "plans-of-care." The hospice patients, along with their families and their friends, needed me to share my expertise/experience in loss, grief, and mourning with them. They needed to hear words from someone who had walked a similar path as their own and who had felt many of their same feelings. They wanted to meet someone who knew what it was like to think thoughts like they were thinking and had asked many of the same questions they were asking. There were people all around me that needed to hear (and see) that death didn't have to mean *The End.* That morning, as I looked out that window, I did not know what my future would look like, but I knew that I would have one. I thought to myself: *There is Life yet to be Lived! … **The River Still Flows.***

I turned in my chair, picked up a pen, and wrote the words on a piece of paper. I took that piece of paper and fastened it to the bulletin board above my workspace at just about eye level. That piece of paper, with those words… ***The River Still Flows….*** stayed on that bulletin board, just about eye level, for many years. Every time I glanced at it, I was reminded that no matter what I faced in life, no matter what I went through (or didn't go through), no matter how I felt (or didn't feel), and no matter what I thought (or didn't think), *There is always life yet to be lived!*

Cogitation: Sometimes we focus so long on what we don't have, we lose sight of what we do have.

Looking at it now, I understand that Bee's death was not a tragic end; it was a brand-new beginning. Instead of coming to the "end of the road," I found myself starting a new adventure. In many ways, the years since her death have been the most rewarding and fulfilling years of my life. I miss her every day, but... *The River Still Flows.*

⌒ ℯ ⌒

Take a Look with Me

One month after Bee's death, I rented a bright red Mustang and made a road trip to visit my brother Brant and his wife, Judy, who live in Spartanburg, South Carolina. I purposefully chose the long route to get there, which took me through the heart of the Smoky Mountains. The fall foliage was breathtakingly beautiful, and the long hours of "windshield time" was therapeutic for me... *The River Still Flows.*

Two months after Bee's death, Ruth married her high school sweetheart, Logan. As we walked together down the aisle, Ben and the ensemble he had assembled softly played music he had arranged. The crowd was on their feet as we slowly made our way to the altar. When we drew close to one of the front pews, Ruth and I paused. There was an empty seat. Ruth gently laid a rose down. Everyone took a deep breath, shed a tear, and the ceremony continued. (One year later, Ben would follow his sister's lead and marry the love of his life, Amber) ... *The River Still Flows.*

Three months after Bee's death, I decorated the house for Christmas. Bee had always loved to turn our house into a winter wonderland. That year I didn't have the energy to go all-out, however, I couldn't stand the idea of not doing anything. I compromised by turned the dining room into my "Christmas room" with trees in every corner and special holiday décor covering the dining table... *The River Still Flows.*

Four months after Bee's death, I faced a decision. New Year's Eve was Bee's birthday, and I did not want to sit around the house waiting to see what direction my feelings and emotions would take me. I decided to go to Katy, Texas, and attend "watch night" services with my friend Albert. I began the New Year of 2012 with prayer... *The River Still Flows.*

Five months after Bee's death, I was at work on Valentine's Day. I had not expected this to be a problem, but as the day went on, florists from all over the city kept coming to deliver bouquets of fresh flowers to my co-workers. By noon, "Valentine's Day" was unavoidable, and everywhere I looked, I was reminded of the loss of *my love*. Finally, I went to my boss and told her, "I will see you tomorrow," drove home, and struggled through the rest of the day alone… *The River Still Flows*.

Six months after Bee's death, I had lunch with someone other than my children. I loved my kids, and we had grown very close after our loss, but I developed a desire to have an adult conversation. The "someone" I shared lunch with happened to be a lady I had known for a number of years. She was the lead teller at Texas Bank and Trust, where my uncle was the CEO. Betty had lost her husband a few years earlier due to Alzheimer's. It turns out that she and I had a lot in common. As time rolled on, we found ourselves falling in love. I had been looking for a friend to eat lunch with, and to my surprise, I found a wonderful wife… *The River Still Flows*.

And so, the story goes on, because there is always *Life yet to be Lived*, and… *The River Still Flows*. Professionally, it was my honor and privilege to represent the Bereavement Department of The Hospice of East Texas for the next eight years. During that time, I was responsible for the follow-up/support of people who had experienced the death of someone special in their lives. It was not unusual for us to average between 40-50 deaths per week. Over eight years that adds up to around 20,000 deaths that I was connected with in some small way or another. Cards, letters, phone calls, and material containing grief information/education were extended to every family. I traveled throughout the 23-county area (15,000 square miles) that The Hospice of East Texas covered: meeting people in their homes, visiting with them at fast-food restaurants, facilitating support groups, conducting seminars, and speaking to groups ranging from garden clubs to quilting clubs. A vast variety of churches invited me to speak to members of their congregations on the subject of grief and loss. Hospitals, cancer treatment centers, and nursing facilities gave me the opportunity to share my experience in caregiving with both families as well as staff, especially during the holidays. There were also children's support groups and day camps to oversee and participate in. Each bereavement service was made available to anyone who wanted to attend whether they had been on hospice service or not, and it was all offered free of charge.

Over the years, the bereavement department continued to develop and expand grief education/ support offerings. Eventually, I was promoted to Director of Care Support and was given charge of not only Bereavement services, but Chaplain, and Volunteer services as well. Regardless of the title, in my view the mission of The Hospice of East Texas, and my job in particular, was to be available for people who were going through a very hard time in life and offer them access to resources that would help them along the way. It was my responsibility to do whatever I could to make what was **hard...** a little **softer.** I knew that I could not make it *easier*, but if I could help make it *softer,* then I felt that I had fulfilled my role. To walk with someone who is walking through *"the Valley of the Shadow of Death"* is perhaps the highest calling of all. Today, I am forever humbled by and thankful for that call.

People would often ask me, "How do you do what you do after all you went through with Bee?" My answer was, "Every time I visit with someone else about their loss, I am reminded of my own. When people tell me their story, it gives me the occasion to share bits and pieces of my own. Almost daily, I am afforded the unique and highly valuable opportunity to stay in touch with feelings and emotions as they relate to Bee's death." My role in caring for others has challenged me to be consistently self-reflective, introspective, and purposefully aware of my own personal grief experience. For me, it has proven to be a very important part of the healing process.

That healing process begins when we recognize the need to begin the healing process. Emotional and spiritual wounds are much like physical wounds, in that they should be attended to, not ignored. At the very least, the wound should be cleaned and dressed properly. The dressing should be changed on a regular basis and appropriate medication should be administered. If complications come, and the wound gets infected, the problem, as well as the source of the problem, needs to be addressed. Given enough time, and with proper attention, the swelling will go down, the pain will become less intense, and the cut will begin to close, i.e., ***the wound will heal***. Remember, one of the worst things to do when wounded is refusing to acknowledge the obvious and choosing to continue as if nothing has happened.

Dealing with loss and the "grief wounds" that go with it is not usually a pleasant thing to do. However, pleasant or not, "It" must be dealt with sooner or later. To ignore "It" is to postpone the pain. To cling to "It" is to prolong the pain. You're not wrong to feel awkward after the loss. It's natural to feel the sting of pain. It's normal to want to "hunker down" and wait for the grief to just go-away. But, think back (turn back) to the beginning of the book. Remember the ***"Popcorn, Potatoes, and the Pomegranates."*** Recognize the *irreversible transformation* that has taken place in your world. Be pro-active, and look for ways to avoid the dreaded *"Boil-over."* Take time to lift the lid and stir things up. Also, as you continue to live from day-to-day, be reminded that when it comes to the grieving process, *small bites* are much more efficient and far more pleasant than big ones. Think: One Bite at a Time! And finally, give yourself permission to feel what you're feeling, and try not to worry about what you are not feeling.

Always be encouraged; look for and pursue healthy new ways to live *your life… your way. Life as it is Now! YES… There is Life yet to be Lived… The River Still Flows.*

COGITATION

"Rather than focusing on what we cannot do… i.e., stop death, stop feeling emotions, or answer all of life's questions… maybe we should focus on what we can do: admit death is a natural part of life, and make preparation for that last creative act. Let us remember that the word 'end' not only refers to a conclusion; it also speaks of a goal. The choices we make in life influence how that goal is attained."

–To Die with Style! *by Marjorie Casebier McCoy*

"I can do everything that I need to do, because the strength of Jesus Christ flows to me, and through me." (Philippians 4:13, paraphrased)

REFLECTION:

Sliding Down a Slide

When was the last time you slid down a slide?

I think back on clear autumn days and trips to the park. The air is clean, clear, and cool. The leaves on the trees are beginning to turn different shades of gold and red and orange. A few lazily float to the ground. As I take in the beauty and my heart begins to warm with thoughts of days gone by, my ears hear the squeals and laughter of children playing. My attention turns to the playground, and I find myself transported in time back to earlier, simpler days. There are swing sets standing ready to take me on a trip gliding up and down. There is a merry-go-round ready to take me around and around. There is a castle or a fort or a ship or a tree house or an airplane... a magical structure that I can pretend in, as I climb on and around and over. Oh, to be a child again.

Somewhere amidst all this fun and excitement and imagination stands the slide. I remember how tall the ladder seemed to me when I was just a little tot. I remember cautiously making the climb to the top of the platform, my trembling, tender hands gripping tightly to the cool metal rail. I remember the lump in my throat and the knot in my stomach as I got to the top. The view was amazing. It seemed like I was on top of a high mountain. Then I would look down. The slide would be shining in the sunshine, and I would hesitate for a moment as I thought about the adventure that was just ahead. A moment of fear, a moment of question, a moment of apprehension...

should I try to turn around and climb down the ladder or go for it? All I had to do was to let go of the sides and enjoy to trip. I take a deep breath and... Whoosh! The thrill of the slide down the slide!

As you walk through the world of grief, you might find yourself facing situations that cause you hesitation. Moments in life when you pause and try to decide whether or not you really want to let go and experience the "slide." Especially during the upcoming holiday season, when you are surrounded by laughter and smiles. It seems like all the stories have a happy ending and everyone is getting what they wish for. All the while your heart aches from the loss of the one you love. With so much "cheer" around, you may feel grumpy, awkward, frustrated, sad, or even a little bitter or jealous. These feelings, as well as countless others, are all normal pieces of your individual grief puzzle. Instinctively you know that you can't go back down the ladder. However, sitting on the top of the slide will not make the feelings disappear. The fact is, the longer you sit there the more intense the feelings can get.

My suggestion... accept your feelings, understand that where you are can be a scary place to be, and that it will require some courage to let go. But remember, as difficult it has been for you to get to where you are and as intimidating the next step may be, there is still a special thrill in store when you choose to let go and slide down that slide. Whoosh!

When was the last time you slid down a slide?

GRIEF TIPS

I offer the following collection of ideas/suggestions to people who are dealing with the pain of death and loss. I have shared these thoughts countless times over the years through my ministry with The Hospice of East Texas. They are presented in no particular order. The following are a combination of ideas that have been shared with a great number of people over the different kinds of losses which elicit different kinds of responses, so not all of the ideas will fit everyone. Likewise, no two people grieve alike; what works for one may not work for another. Treat this list for what it is: a gathering of assorted suggestions that various people have tried with success. Perhaps what helped them work through their grief will help you. The emphasis here is upon specific, practical ideas. Think of them as "tools in your toolbox."

Talk regularly with a friend. Talking with another person about what you think and feel is one of the best things you can do for yourself.

Walk. Go for walks outside every day if you can. Don't overdo it, but walk briskly enough that it feels invigorating.

Carry or wear a linking object. Carry something in your pocket or purse that reminds you of the one who died.

Visit the grave. Not all people prefer to do this. But if it feels right to you, then do so.

Create a memory book. Compile photographs that document your loved one's life. Arrange them into some sort of order so they tell a story. Reminisce as you do so.

Recall your dreams. Your dreams often have important things to say about your feelings and about your relationship with the one who died.

Tell people what helps you and what doesn't. People around you may not understand what you need, so tell them.

Write things down. Most people who are grieving become more forgetful than usual. Help yourself remember what you want by keeping track of it on paper or with whatever system works best for you.

Ask for a copy of the memorial service. If the funeral liturgy or memorial service held special meaning for you because of what was spoken or read, ask for the words.

Remember the Serenity Prayer. "God, grant me the serenity to accept the things I cannot change, courage to change the things I can, and the wisdom to know one from the other."

Plant something living as a memorial. Plant a flower, a bush, or a tree in memory of the one who died. Do this ceremonially if you wish, perhaps with others present.

Plan at least one thing you'll do each day. Even if your grief is very painful and your energy is very low, plan to complete at least one thing each day, even if it's a small thing.

Spend time in your loved one's space. If it's what you want to do, you may sit in the other's favorite chair, lie in their bed, smell their clothes or things, or just stand in their room or among their possessions.

Journal. Write out your thoughts and feelings. Do this whenever you feel the urge, but do it at least several times a week, if not several times a day.

Rest. Grieving is hard work. Do what is best for you. GET YOUR REST! Take naps if you wish.

Purchase something soft to sleep with. A teddy bear is a favorite choice for some, but there are other options. Select something that feels warm and cuddly. Then, whatever your age, cuddle it.

Write to the person who died. Write letters or other messages to your loved one. They may be gone physically, but they are still a part of your life.

Get a physical. It is wise to have a physical examination within a few months after the death. It is also an assuring thing to do.

Consider joining a support group. Spending time with a small group of people who have undergone a similar life experience can be very therapeutic.

If you like animals, get a pet. A pet can provide attention and affection in a way that may help you adapt to the loss of attention and affection you are experiencing after this significant person has died.

Light a candle at mealtime. Especially if you eat alone, but even if you don't, consider lighting a taper at the table in memory of your loved one. Pause to remember them as you light it.

Donate their possessions meaningfully. Whether you give your loved one's personal possessions to someone you know or to a stranger, find ways to pass these things along so that others might benefit from them.

Create a memory area in your home. In a space that feels appropriate, arrange a small table or shelf that honors the person: a framed photograph or two, perhaps a prized possession or award, a bottle of perfume/cologne, or something they created or cherished.

Drink water. Grieving people can easily become dehydrated. Crying can naturally lead to that. Make this one easy way that you can care for yourself.

Use your hands. Sometimes there is value in doing repetitive things with your hands, something you don't have to think about very much because it becomes second nature. Knitting, crocheting, or whittling are good examples.

Give yourself respites from your grief. There is value in sometimes consciously deciding that you'll think about something else for a while, or that you'll do something you've always enjoyed doing.

See a grief counselor. If you are concerned about how you're feeling and how well you're adapting, make an appointment with a counselor who specializes in grief.

Begin your day with your loved one. If your grief is young, you'll probably wake up thinking of that person anyway. Focus this time in a positive way.

Invite someone to be your telephone buddy. If your grief and sadness hit you especially hard at times and you have no one nearby to turn to, ask someone you trust to be your telephone "go to" person.

Avoid certain people if you need to. If there are

people in your life who make it difficult for you to do your grieving, then do what you can to stay out of their way.

Structure alone time. If you're often among family, friends, and colleagues, make sure you also have time by yourself.

Listen to music. Choose music you believe will help you at a given moment. Let the sounds surround you and soothe you.

Create your own music. Play an instrument. Sing a song. Hum. Use your music to express what you feel, to unite you to others, to focus on your hope.

Do something you're loved one would enjoy. Remember the one who died in your own unique way.

Write stories about your loved one. Recreate those events that you don't want to forget. Write them down in detail.

Screen your entertainment. Some TV shows and/ or movies are best not viewed when you are in deep grief. The same goes for certain books and articles. (For example, if your loved one recently died of cancer, you might think twice before you relive that experience on a 30-foot movie screen.)

Read practical books and articles on grief. Reading is a great way to find your way through this roundabout experience.

Engage your soul. Don't neglect the spiritual aspect of grief. Think about spiritual things, pray, and give yourself permission to ask spiritual questions.

Change some things. As soon as it seems right, alter some things in your home to make clear this significant change that has occurred in your life.

Allow yourself to laugh. Sometimes you'll recall something hilarious that happened in the past. When that happens, go ahead and LAUGH!

Allow yourself to cry. Crying goes naturally with grief. A good rule of thumb is this: if you feel like crying, then cry. If you do not, then don't.

Talk with the one who died. If it helps, you might "talk with" the one who died. This inclination to converse will eventually go away, when the time is right.

Donate in your loved one's name. Honor the memory of the one you love by giving a gift or gifts to a cause that is connected to them in a special way.

Create/Commission a memory quilt. Put together a wall hanging or a bedroom quilt that recalls important events in the life of the one who died.

Plant yourself in nature. Dig a flower garden and keep it in color as long as possible. Dig a vegetable garden and stay close to it until frost. Walk in the forest. Collect leaves and wildflowers. Watch how rivers and lakes and oceans behave. Look up at the stars in the night skies and reflect.

Plan ahead for Special Days. Special events and dates can be difficult times, especially for the first year or two. Give thought beforehand and plan ahead. Make a list and prioritize. Avoid making last-minute decisions under pressure. Set your own holiday tone. Set realistic limits for yourself. Seek a balance between quiet time and time spent with others. Think about what kind of celebration is best for you. You may want to change things up this year, and if you do, remember you can change them again next year. State your needs/desires clearly to others. It's okay to say "no" and to qualify "yes." Feel free to express your emotions and to talk about the one who has died. Take time to acknowledge and honor the one you love. Allow others to grieve differently than you. Expect the best. Expecting the best is the first step in experiencing the best!

As you continue this journey... remember: Be patient with yourself. Learn how to ask for and accept help. Permit yourself to feel your own feelings. Rather than running from it, lean into the pain. Be good to yourself. Hold on to Hope. Look for Happiness. Embrace Love.

1 John 4:8 ... God is Love.

ABOUT THE AUTHOR

Wes M. Bynum began his journey of compassion and service when he was ordained in 1981 as a minister with the Assemblies of God Church. He served as a pastor in local congregations for 25 years. Wes and his first wife, Bee, began volunteering with The Hospice of East Texas, not realizing they would one day become the beneficiary of others' kindness when Bee was diagnosed with cancer. After her diagnosis, Wes entered the Clinical Pastor Education (CPE) program at Trinity Mother Frances hospital in Tyler, Texas. The year-long residency is offered to ministers who have a heartfelt desire to serve as chaplains in a clinical setting. Wes completed his coursework and became a chaplain in 2011, the same year Bee died at the age of 51. He served on staff with The Hospice of East Texas to continue his focus on families who lose a loved one.

Wes served as a chaplain for The Hospice of East Texas and eventually became Director of Care Support Services to help other families navigate the difficult and complex experience of grief. As Director, he oversaw 23 counties and was responsible for ensuring the care and follow up of upwards of 300 patients every day. Wes led seminars on grief for patient families and counseled with countless loved ones in an effort to allow God's love to flow freely from him to others in need.

Wes retired in 2020 after 25 years of combined service and currently serves as a Care Support Consultant, making himself available as needed. Wes married Betty in 2012, who lost her first husband to early-onset Alzheimer's disease in 2009 at the age of 57. Wes and Betty are both retired and spend their time serving others in ministry and enjoying life in East Texas.